Company's Coming

®

Jean Paré's Favorites
Volume One

FRONT COVER PHOTO

1. Raspberry Satin page 135
2. Raspberry Sauce page 135
3. Chocolate Leaves page 135

BACK COVER PHOTO

1. Tomato Dumplings page 62
2. Vegetable Dish page 76
3. Chinese Pepper Steak on Rice page 63
4. Orange Almond Salad page 153

Company's Coming

Jean Paré's Favorites
Volume One

Copyright © 1988 by Company's Coming Publishing Limited
All Rights Reserved

First Edition September, 1988

I.S.B.N. 0-9690695-9-6

Published and Distributed Simultaneously
in Canada and the United States by
Company's Coming Publishing Limited
Box 8037, Station "F"
Edmonton, Alberta, Canada
T6H 4N9

Printed in Canada

Family, friends, cooking . . . these are my favorites.

table of Contents

Foreword

"How many cookbooks will you write?" From the beginning of my career as an author, I have been asked that question. Ten seemed to be a reasonable estimate in the early years, but it is now obvious to me that there is no end in sight.

Tenth in the Company's Coming series, JEAN PARÉ'S FAVORITES VOLUME ONE is a collection of my favorite recipes from the first nine books and a sprinkling of seventy-five previously unpublished recipes. New recipes are designated by a star in the index. The result is a special collector's edition hard cover book, designed to commemorate the Company's Coming cookbook series. You will recognize the familiar format and can rest assured that each page adheres to my standard of easy-to-follow recipes, requiring mostly common affordable ingredients. And the book lies flat too — a must for the kitchen!

Many of the recipes included in this book are old family favorites —some dating back to the nineteenth century. As in your family, good cooking stands the test of time. I encourage you to search out the recipes of your parents and grandparents as I have done. Hour upon hour I have pored over those priceless heirlooms. Today, I am proud to share them with you. So please, taste the tradition.

Jean Paré

Jean Paré was born and raised during the Great Depression in Irma, a small farm town in eastern Alberta. Jean grew up understanding that the combination of family, friends and home cooking is the essence of a good life. Jean learned from her mother, Ruby Elford, to appreciate good cooking and was encouraged by her father, Edward Elford, who praised even her earliest attempts. When she left home she took with her many acquired family recipes, her love of cooking and her intriguing desire to read recipe books like novels!

While raising a family of four, Jean was always busy in her kitchen preparing delicious, tasty treats and savory meals for family and friends of all ages. Her reputation flourished as the mom who would happily feed the neighborhood.

In 1963, when her four children had all reached school age, Jean volunteered to cater to the 50th anniversary of the Vermilion School of Agriculture, now Lakeland College. Working out of her home, Jean prepared a dinner for over 1000 people which launched a flourishing catering operation that continued for over eighteen years. During this time she was provided with countless opportunities to test new ideas with immediate feedback —resulting in empty plates and contented customers! Whether preparing cocktail sandwiches for a house party or serving a hot meal for 1500 people, Jean Paré earned a reputation for good food, courteous service and reasonable prices.

"Why don't you write a cookbook?" Time and again Jean was asked that question as requests for her recipes mounted. Jean's response was to team up with her son Grant Lovig in the fall of 1980 to form Company's Coming Publishing Limited. April 14, 1981 marked the debut of "150 DELICIOUS SQUARES", the first Company's Coming cookbook in what soon would become Canada's most popular cookbook series. Jean released a new title each year for the first six years. The pace quickened and by 1987 the company had begun publishing two titles each year.

Jean Paré's operation has grown from the early days of working out of a spare bedroom in her home to operating a large and fully equipped test kitchen in Vermilion, near the home she and her husband Larry built. Full time staff has grown steadily to include marketing personnel located in major cities across Canada and the United States. Home Office is located in Edmonton, Alberta where distribution, accounting and administration functions are headquartered.

Jean Paré's approach to cooking has always called for easy-to-follow recipes using mostly common, affordable ingredients. Her wonderful collection of time-honored recipes, many of which are family heirlooms, are a welcome addition to any kitchen. That's why we say: taste the tradition.

ARTICHOKE SQUARES

You will want to keep a container of artichoke hearts on the shelf to make these uncommon appetizers. Very tasty.

Butter or margarine	1 tbsp.	15 mL
Finely chopped onion	¾ cup	175 mL
Garlic cloves, minced	1 - 2	1 - 2
Eggs	4	4
Grated medium Cheddar cheese	2 cups	500 mL
Dry bread crumbs, fine	¼ cup	60 mL
Parsley flakes	2 tsp.	10 mL
Salt	¼ tsp.	1 mL
Pepper	⅛ tsp.	0.5 mL
Oregano	⅛ tsp.	0.5 mL
Cayenne pepper	⅛ tsp.	0.5 mL
Marinated artichoke hearts, drained and chopped	2 x 6 oz.	2 x 170 mL

Put butter, onion and garlic into frying pan. Sauté until clear and soft.

Beat eggs until frothy. Add remaining ingredients. Add onion mixture. Mix well. Turn into greased 9 x 9 inch (22 x 22 cm) pan. Bake in 325° F (160° C) oven for about 30 minutes until set. Cool and cut into squares. May also be served hot. Makes 36.

Pictured on page 17.

ORANGE JULIUS

A healthy milkshake for everyone.

Frozen concentrated orange juice	6 oz.	170 mL
Milk	1 cup	250 mL
Water	1 cup	250 mL
Egg	1	1
Granulated sugar	2 tbsp.	30 mL
Vanilla	2 tsp.	10 mL
Ice cubes	12	12

Put orange concentrate into blender. Add next 5 ingredients. May be made this far ahead of time. To serve, add ice cubes. Blend until ice is gone. Serve immediately. Makes 5 cups (1.25 L).

Pictured on page 35.

SHRIMP QUICHE

A real treat for either expected or unexpected company. A good freezer delicacy. Great evening snack as well as pre-dinner.

Pastry, your own or a mix

Canned broken shrimp, small size	4 oz.	113 g
Finely chopped onion	¼ cup	50 mL
Shredded Swiss cheese	1 cup	250 mL
Eggs	2	2
Mayonnaise	½ cup	125 mL
Milk	⅓ cup	75 mL
Salt	¼ tsp.	1 mL
Dried dill weed	¼ tsp.	1 mL

Line 12 muffin cups with pastry. Set aside.

Rinse and drain shrimp and divide equally among pastry shells. Divide onion next followed by the Swiss cheese.

Beat eggs until frothy. Add mayonnaise, milk, salt and dill weed. Beat to mix. Pour over top of shrimp mixture in shells. Bake in 400° F (220° C) oven for 15 to 20 minutes until nicely browned. Serve warm. Makes 12.

Pictured on page 17.

CRAB WONTONS

These can be held in the refrigerator and deep-fried at the last minute or they can be deep-fried ahead of time and reheated at the last minute. Either way, you will need to make lots.

Crab	4¾ oz.	135 g
Cream cheese, room temperature	8 oz.	250 g
Green onions, finely chopped	2	2
Salt	¼ tsp.	1 mL
Wonton wrappers	1 lb.	454 g
Fat for deep-frying		

(continued on next page)

In medium size bowl mix crab with cream cheese. Add onion and salt. Mix well.

Place 1 tsp. (5 mL) in center of wonton wrapper. Moisten edges. Fold over, forming triangle. Press edges to seal. Fold 2 corners over, moisten and press together to seal.

Deep-fry a few at a time, turning to brown both sides, in hot fat 375° F (190° C). Drain on paper towels. Serve immediately or cool and store in covered container in refrigerator with waxed paper between layers.

To serve, arrange on baking sheet. Heat in 350° F (180° C) oven for about 15 minutes until hot. Good served with Apricot Sauce, page 25. Makes 4 to 5 dozen.

Note: Uncooked wontons may be frozen in a single layer, then bagged. Thaw before deep-frying.

Pictured on page 17.

CHILI CON QUESO

Chilee-cahn-KAY-soh is a mild cream cheese dip served warm with tortilla chips. Just as delicious with potato chips. Excellent.

Velveeta cheese	1 lb.	500 g
Light cream	1 cup	250 mL
Can of chopped green chilies	4 oz.	114 g
Finely chopped green pepper	¼ cup	50 mL
Chopped pimiento	4 tsp.	20 mL

Cut Velveeta cheese into chunks into a heavy saucepan or top of a double boiler. Add cream and chopped chilies. Cook green pepper 2 minutes on high power in microwave or boil until tender crisp. Add to cheese mixture along with pimiento. Melt together stirring frequently. Heat slowly. If heated too fast or too hot, cheese may go stringy. Serve warm with tortilla chips. Your own are best. Better to make a day ahead so flavors blend. Makes 3 cups (700 mL).

CHILI CON QUESO SAUCE: Pour over enchiladas, burritos, and any other food that a good sauce enhances.

Note: If Velveeta is not available, use another mild, soft, process cheese.

Note: To thicken, mix 1 tbsp. (15 mL) water with 1 tbsp. (15 mL) cornstarch and add to hot sauce. Stir until bubbly hot.

BROCCOLI DIP

A good mild dip.

Frozen chopped broccoli	10 oz.	284 mL
Finely chopped onion	1 cup	250 mL
Butter or margarine	½ cup	125 mL
Condensed cream of mushroom soup	10 oz.	284 mL
Mushroom stems and pieces, drained, reserve juice	10 oz.	284 mL
Dash of cayenne pepper		
Potato, corn or taco chips		

Cook broccoli as package directs. Drain. Set aside.

Sauté onion in butter until clear and soft.

Stir in soup. Chop mushrooms and add along with cayenne pepper. Add broccoli. For a thinner dip, stir in reserved mushroom juice to desired consistency.

Serve hot with chips.

SPINACH BITES

Spinach will never be more in vogue than in these delicious appetizers.

Frozen spinach, chopped, cooked and drained	10 oz.	284 g
Prepared bread stuffing	1½ cups	350 mL
Finely chopped onion	¾ cup	175 mL
Grated Parmesan cheese	¼ cup	50 mL
Garlic salt	1 tsp.	5 mL
Thyme	¼ tsp.	1 mL
Pepper	¼ tsp.	1 mL
Eggs, beaten	3	3
Butter or margarine, melted	⅓ cup	75 mL

Mix all ingredients together. Let stand for moisture to absorb. Add more crumbs if needed. Shape into 1 inch (2.5 cm) balls. Arrange on greased baking sheet. Bake in 350°F (180°C) oven for about 20 minutes. May be stored in refrigerator or freezer before baking. Thaw before baking. Makes 2½ dozen.

Pictured on page 17.

One of the best. Hold in refrigerator until ready to broil.

Mushrooms, medium large	24	24
Butter or margarine	3 tbsp.	50 mL
Finely chopped onion	1 cup	250 mL
Ground beef	¼ lb.	115 g
Finely chopped celery	2 tbsp.	30 mL
Mushroom stems, finely chopped		
Ketchup	¼ cup	50 mL
Dry bread crumbs	¼ cup	50 mL
Garlic powder	1 tsp.	5 mL
Salt	½ tsp.	2 mL
Pepper	½ tsp.	2 mL
Grated Parmesan cheese	¼ cup	50 mL
Grated mozzarella cheese (optional)	½ cup	125 mL

Remove stems from mushrooms with a gentle twist. Reserve.

Melt butter in frying pan. Add onion, ground beef and celery. Fry until onion is clear and soft and beef is nicely browned.

Add next 6 ingredients. Stir well. Remove from heat. Stuff mushroom caps. Arrange on baking sheet.

Sprinkle with Parmesan cheese, then with mozzarella, if you wish. Place on second rack from broiler. Broil for about 5 minutes, until heated through. Serve hot. Makes 24.

Note: If using small mushrooms, omit mozzarella and place a few shreds on each cap, otherwise it will topple off.

Pictured on page 17.

Paré Pointer

It would be great if a cold war meant a snowball fight.

CRAB MOUSSE

So festive when served with tiny toast cups piled around. Supply a knife so guests can help themselves.

Cold water	¼ cup	50 mL
Unflavored gelatin	¼ oz.	7 g
Condensed cream of mushroom soup	10 oz.	284 mL
Cream cheese, softened	8 oz.	250 mL
Mayonnaise	⅔ cup	150 mL
Finely chopped celery	¾ cup	175 mL
Canned crabmeat (or fresh, cooked)	5 oz.	142 g
Worcestershire sauce	1½ tsp.	7 mL
Dry onion flakes	1 tsp.	5 mL

Put cold water into saucepan. Sprinkle gelatin over top. Let stand for 5 minutes.

Add mushroom soup, cheese and mayonnaise. Heat and stir until dissolved and melted. Remove from heat. Chill until it begins to thicken.

Add celery. Drain crab and remove membrane. Add crabmeat, Worcestershire sauce and onion. Stir well. Pour into 2 cup (500 mL) mold. Chill. To serve, unmold on serving dish. Surround with Toast Cups, below, and/or crackers. Serves 15 to 20.

Pictured on page 17.

TOAST CUPS

These are so easy to make yet look so special.

White bread slices	12	12

Cut crusts from sandwich loaf bread. Cut each slice into 4 squares. Press into small ungreased muffin cups. A small empty muffin cup that holds 4 tsp. (20 mL) is a good size. Bake in 350°F (180°C) oven on bottom rack for about 15 minutes until corners are well browned. Turn pan over to remove toast cups. Cool completely. Store in plastic bag. To serve, fill with filling or pile cups around filling. Makes 48.

Pictured on page 17.

MUSHROOM SPREAD

May also be used as a dip. A bit unusual. A good mock caviar.

Butter or margarine	2 tbsp.	30 mL
Finely chopped onion	¾ cup	175 mL
Fresh mushrooms, finely chopped	1 cup	225 mL
Paprika	1½ tsp.	7 mL
Sour cream	½ cup	125 mL
Lemon juice	1 tbsp.	15 mL
Salt	¼ tsp.	1 mL
Dry dill weed	¼ tsp.	1 mL
Pepper, light sprinkle		
Chives		

Melt butter in frying pan. Add onion. Sauté 2 to 3 minutes.

Add mushrooms and paprika. Sauté 3 to 4 minutes.

Stir in sour cream, lemon juice, salt, dill weed and pepper.

Serve hot, sprinkled with chives, along with crackers, Toast Cups (page 14) or black bread.

Pictured on page 17.

SHRIMP SPREAD

Consider your heart won when you sample this. Expect rave reviews.

Mayonnaise	½ cup	125 mL
Butter (not margarine)	½ cup	125 mL
Canned broken shrimp, drained	2 x 4 oz.	2 x 113 g
Minced onion	1 tbsp.	15 mL
Garlic powder	⅛ tsp.	0.5 mL
Lemon juice	1 tbsp.	15 mL

Cream mayonnaise and butter. Add shrimp, onion, garlic powder and lemon juice. Mix and press into dish for serving. Butter firms more than margarine when chilled and that is a requirement in this recipe. Chill. Serve with crackers, Toast Cups (page 14) or flatbread. Makes about 2 cups (500 mL).

Pictured on page 17.

VEGETABLE DIP

A dip made of vegetables. It has a very slight flavor of green pepper. One of the best.

Medium onion	½	½
Medium carrot	½	½
Green pepper	½	½
Vinegar	2 tbsp.	30 mL
Salad dressing such as Miracle Whip	1 cup	250 mL
Process cheese spread such as Cheese Whiz	½ cup	125 mL

Assorted fresh vegetables, cut small, mushrooms, broccoli, radishes, pepper rings, celery, cauliflower, zucchini

Measure first 5 ingredients into blender. Blend until smooth.

Add cheese and purée. Chill. It will thicken when chilled. Serve with vegetables. Makes 2 cups (500 mL).

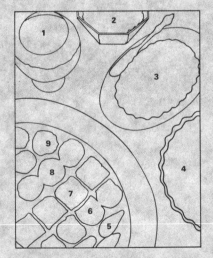

You will never go wrong serving this. Positively everyone's favorite.

Thick sirloin steak	1½ lb.	750 mL
Soy sauce	¾ cup	150 mL
Brown sugar, packed	½ cup	125 mL
Cooking oil	2 tbsp.	30 mL
Garlic powder (or 1 clove, minced)	¼ tsp.	1 mL
Ginger powder	½ tsp.	2 mL

Wooden skewers (soaked in water to prevent scorching)

Slice steak about ⅛ inch (.5 cm) thick to make long thin slices. If meat is partially frozen, it is much easier to do.

In bowl, with tight-fitting cover, mix soy sauce, sugar, oil, garlic powder and ginger powder. Put meat into bowl. Press down to cover with marinade. Allow to marinate for at least ½ hour.

Thread meat on skewers accordian-fashion. Broil only until medium-rare. Store, covered in refrigerator. To serve, pile on baking sheet. Heat in 400°F (200°C) oven for about 5 minutes or until hot.

Note: If you have no skewers, slice meat thinly, then into squares. Marinate as above. Transfer meat with slotted spoon to pan with sides. Broil, 1 layer deep, on 1 side only until sizzling and cooked to medium-rare stage. Cool a bit then store in refrigerator. To serve, heat in covered casserole in 350°F (180°C) oven for about 20 minutes or until hot. Serve with picks. Delicious. Serves 12.

Note: Peanut sauce is often poured over satay before serving.

SATAY WITH PINEAPPLE: Thread 2 marinated and broiled meat squares on pick with pineapple chunk in between. Bake as above.

Fare Pointer

The real reason the three little pigs left home was because their father was such a bore.

TINY PIZZAS

A several-bite finger food that the whole crowd will love.

All-purpose flour	1½ cups	375 mL
Granulated sugar	1 tbsp	15 mL
Baking powder	1 tbsp.	15 mL
Salt	½ tsp.	2 mL
Cooking oil	¼ cup	50 mL
Milk	½ cup	125 mL

Combine flour, sugar, baking powder and salt in bowl. Stir well.

Add oil and milk. Mix into ball, adding a bit more milk if needed to make a soft dough. Roll about ¼ inch (1 cm) thick on lightly floured board. Cut into 2½ inch (6 cm) rounds. Cover with topping. Makes 18.

TOPPING

Tomato sauce	3 tbsp.	50 mL
Oregano, sprinkle		
Pepperoni slices (optional)	54 - 72	54 - 72
Mozzarella cheese slices, quartered (or use shredded)	5	5

Spread ½ tsp. (2 mL) tomato sauce over each pizza followed with a sprinkle of oregano. Put about 3 to 4 slices of pepperoni on each. Top with mozzarella cheese. Arrange on ungreased baking pan. Bake in 400° F (200° C) oven for 10 to 12 minutes until browned.

When you're run down the best thing to take is the number of the car that hit you.

DILLY DIP

About the best all-round never-get-tired-of-dip you will find. A good spur-of-the-moment choice. Equally good with vegetables or chips. A real standby.

Mayonnaise	1 cup	250 mL
Sour cream	1 cup	250 mL
Dry onion flakes	2 tsp.	10 mL
Dry parsley flakes	2 tsp.	10 mL
Dry dill weed	2 tsp.	10 mL
Seasoned salt	1 tsp.	5 mL
Monosodium glutamate (optional)	1 tsp.	5 mL

Mix all ingredients in bowl. Chill. Serve with potato chips, broccoli, cauliflower, mushrooms, celery sticks, carrot sticks, bread sticks, radish, cherry tomatoes, green pepper slices and any other vegetable you can think of. Makes 2 cups (500 mL).

JALAPEÑO JELLY

Hahl-ah-PAIN-yoh jelly is different and a treat to eat.

Canned chopped pickled jalapeño peppers (or more)	¼ cup	50 mL
Chopped red pepper	¾ cup	175 mL
White vinegar	1 cup	225 mL
Lemon juice	3 tbsp.	50 mL
Granulated sugar	5 cups	1.1 L
Bottle of Certo	6 oz.	170 g

Put jalapeño and red pepper into blender. Add half of the vinegar. Blend smooth. Pour into large saucepan. Add rest of vinegar, lemon juice and sugar. Bring to boil, stirring often. Boil for 10 minutes. Add Certo. Return to full rolling boil. Boil 1 minute. Remove from heat and skim. Pour into sterilized jars. Seal with melted paraffin. Makes 4 jars, 8 oz. (225 mL) size. Spread crackers with cream cheese and top with jelly.

JALAPEÑO CHEESE: Place cream cheese on shallow plate. Cover with jalapeño jelly. Serve with assorted crackers.

CHILI CHEESE LOG

You will need to make this three or four days ahead to mellow.

Grated Cheddar cheese	3 cups	750 mL
Cream cheese, softened	4 oz.	125 g
Worcestershire sauce	¾ tsp.	3 mL
Garlic salt	½ tsp.	2 mL
Pepper	¼ tsp.	1 mL

Chili powder, lots

Put Cheddar cheese, cream cheese, Worcestershire sauce, garlic salt and pepper into mixing bowl. Beat until soft and smooth. Roll into 2 rolls. Make diameter a bit smaller than round cracker so slices will fit on top.

Sprinkle waxed paper liberally with chili powder. Roll to coat each log well. Wrap in waxed paper. Chill in refrigerator for 3 or 4 days to blend. Put slices on round crackers or serve with a cheese knife and assorted crackers. Freezes well. Makes 4 to 5 dozen slices.

CURRIED CHEESE SPREAD

Delicious. Good on anything!

Cream cheese, softened	8 oz.	250 g
Apricot jam	¼ cup	50 mL
Chopped almonds or cashews, toasted	⅓ cup	75 mL
Curry powder	¼ - ½ tsp.	1 - 2 mL
Dry mustard	¼ tsp.	1 mL

Mash cheese and jam together. Mix in nuts, curry powder and mustard. Add smaller amount of curry first then more if needed. Pack into small bowl. Serve with butter knife and crackers. Makes about 1¼ cups (300 mL).

CURRIED CHEDDAR SPREAD: Substitute 2 cups (500 mL) grated sharp Cheddar cheese for the cream cheese.

CHUTNEY SPREAD: Substitute chutney for the apricot jam.

Note: Toast almonds in 350°F (180°C) oven for about 10 minutes until browned. Stir once or twice.

Always so desirable, these are sure to whet the appetite.

Brown bread slices, day old	4	4
White bread slices, day old	2	2
Butter or margarine, softened		
Ham and egg fillings		

Use 1 white and 2 brown slices per stack. Use 2 different fillings for each stack. Place brown slices on the bottom and top. Butter and spread fillings between each slice. Cut crusts from all sides. Wrap and chill. To serve, slice in ½ inch (1 cm) slices. Then cut each slice into 3 or 4 strips. Repeat with other slices. Makes about 3½ to 5 dozen.

EGG FILLING

Hard-boiled eggs, chopped	6	6
Finely diced celery	2 tbsp.	30 mL
Salt	½ tsp.	2 mL
Parsley flakes	½ tsp.	2 mL
Onion powder	¼ tsp.	1 mL
Salad dressing	¼ cup	50 mL

Mix all together. If too dry, add a bit more salad dressing. Makes about 1¾ cups (400 mL).

HAM FILLING

Flakes of ham	2 x 6.5 oz.	2 x 184 g
Sweet pickle relish	2 tbsp.	30 mL
Onion flakes, crushed	1 tsp.	5 mL
Salad dressing	3 tbsp.	50 mL

Combine ham, relish, onion and salad dressing. If too dry, add a bit more salad dressing. Mash with potato masher until smooth.

Paré Pointer

If you cross a skunk and an eagle you would have something that stunk to high heaven.

SURPRISE SPREAD

Although this looks like a pizza, the surprise is when you find yourself eating it by the spoonful.

Cream cheese, softened	8 oz.	250 mL
Sour cream	½ cup	125 mL
Mayonnaise	¼ cup	50 mL
Canned small or broken shrimp, rinsed and drained	3 x 4 oz.	3 x 113 g
Seafood cocktail sauce	1 cup	250 mL
Shredded mozzarella cheese	2 cups	500 mL
Green pepper, chopped	1	1
Green onions, chopped	3	3
Tomato, diced	1	1

Mix first 3 ingredients together. Spread over 12 inch (30 cm) pizza pan.

Scatter shrimp over cheese mixture. Add layers of seafood sauce, mozzarella cheese, green pepper, onions and tomato. Cover and chill until ready to serve. Supply assorted crackers and spoons for spreading. Toast Cups (page 14) are great. Serves 10 to 12.

Note: Omit 1 can of shrimp if desired. It will still cover quite well.

FROTHY LIME PUNCH

A delight to the eye as well as the palate. No Irish spirits in this!

Pineapple juice	8 cups	2 L
Lime drink mix (see note)	2 env.	2 env.
Granulated sugar	2 cups	450 mL
Lime sherbet	1 qt.	1 L
Seven Up or ginger ale	8 cups	2 L
Whole strawberries for garnish		

Put pineapple juice and lime drink mix into punch bowl. Stir in sugar until dissolved.

Spoon sherbet into punch bowl. Add Seven Up slowly. Let stand 15 minutes.

(continued on next page)

Add a few whole strawberries and serve. Makes about 20 cups (5 L).

Note: Lime drink mix (such as Kool-Aid) comes in envelopes to make 2 quarts (2 L) of liquid when used with water. Presweetened mix may be used. Just omit sugar. Lemon-lime flavor may be used if lime isn't available.

Pictured on page 17.

POLYNESIAN MEATBALLS

A succulent bite — a hit every time. The sauce makes them perfect.

Ground beef	2 lbs.	1 kg
Soy sauce	3 tbsp.	50 mL
Brown sugar (or granulated)	1 tbsp.	15 mL
Water chestnuts, finely chopped	10 oz.	284 mL
Onion powder	½ tsp.	2 mL
Parsley flakes	1 tsp.	5 mL
Garlic powder (or 2 cloves, minced)	½ tsp.	2 mL

Combine all 7 ingredients in large bowl. Mix well. Shape into small bite size balls — at least 40. Place on baking sheet with sides. Bake in 375°F (190°C) oven for about 15 minutes. Serve hot with Apricot Sauce. Supply picks. May be reheated in 400°F (200°C) oven for 5 minutes or until hot. Makes about 4 dozen.

APRICOT SAUCE

Apricot jam	1 cup	250 mL
Cider vinegar	3 tbsp.	50 mL
Paprika	¼ tsp.	1 mL

In small bowl combine jam, vinegar and paprika. Stir well, pour into a pretty bowl and dip in. Just right!

MUSHROOM TURNOVERS

One of the tastiest appetizers ever. May be frozen baked or unbaked. Absolutely delectable.

CREAM CHEESE PASTRY

Cream cheese	8 oz.	250 g
Butter or margarine	½ cup	125 mL
All-purpose flour	1½ cups	375 mL

Have cheese and butter at room temperature. Put into bowl and beat together well. Mix in flour. Shape into ball. Chill at least 1 hour.

FILLING

Butter or margarine	3 tbsp.	50 mL
Large onion, finely chopped	1	1
Fresh mushrooms, chopped	½ lb.	250 g
All-purpose flour	2 tbsp.	30 mL
Salt	1 tsp.	5 mL
Pepper	¼ tsp.	1 mL
Thyme	¼ tsp.	1 mL
Sour cream	¼ cup	50 mL
Egg, beaten	1	1

Combine butter, onion and mushrooms in frying pan. Sauté about 10 minutes until tender.

Add flour, salt, pepper and thyme. Stir together. Add sour cream. Stir until thickened. Remove from heat. Cool thoroughly.

Roll pastry fairly thin. Cut into 3 inch (7.5 cm) rounds. Place 1 tsp. (5 mL) filling in center of each circle. Dampen outer half edge with beaten egg. Fold over and press edges together with fork or fingers to seal. Arrange on greased baking sheet. Cut tiny slits in top of each.

Brush tops with beaten egg. Bake in 450° F (230° C) oven for about 10 minutes or until golden brown. Makes 3 to 4 dozen.

Note: To use canned sliced mushrooms rather than fresh, drain and chop 2 x 10 oz. (284 mL) cans and add to onion. Just as delicious and always on hand.

HAM AND CHEESE BALL

It is easy and convenient to have all of the makings on hand for this good spread.

Cream cheese, softened	8 oz.	250 g
Cans of ham flakes	2 x 6½ oz.	2 x 184 g
Dried chives	2 tsp.	10 mL
Lemon juice	2 tsp.	10 mL
Worcestershire sauce	½ tsp.	2 mL

Parsley, chopped

Beat or mash cheese and ham together until blended. Add chives, lemon juice and Worcestershire sauce. Shape into ball, chilling first if necessary. If too soft, shape into mound on plate.

Roll in parsley. Chill. Serve with crackers. Makes 2½ cups (575 mL).

HAM ROLL CANAPÉS: Form into a roll. Make roll smaller in diameter than your favorite round cracker. To serve, place thin slices on crackers, or use as a spread.

WIENER BITES

These are among the best. You will have to make this in multiple quantities. Freezes well.

Wieners, cut in 6 pieces	8	8
Wide bacon slices (or twice the number of narrow slices)	12	12

Wieners that are 5 inches (13 cm) in length can be cut into 6 pieces each for bite size servings.

Fry bacon slices until fat part has lost its whiteness. Do not fry until crisp or it won't roll. Cut slice in half crosswise and lengthwise. When cool enough to handle, wrap around wiener section and secure with toothpick. Uncooked bacon may be used but it takes longer to cook (they need broiling) at the last minute.

To serve: Arrange on baking tray (or plate for microwave) and heat in hot oven 400° F (200° C) until sizzling hot. Can be kept hot on hot serving tray. Makes 48.

BABY CHEDDAR TARTS

These cute little duffers are every bit as good as they look.

PASTRY

Butter or margarine, softened	½ cup	125 mL
Cream cheese, softened	4 oz.	125 g
All-purpose flour	1 cup	250 mL

Beat butter and cream cheese until smooth and light. Work in flour. Roll into long thin roll. Mark off, then cut into 24 pieces. Press into small tart tins to form shells.

FILLING

Grated Cheddar cheese	1 cup	250 mL
Egg	1	1
Milk	½ cup	125 mL
Salt	¼ tsp.	1 mL
Onion salt	¼ tsp.	1 mL

Divide cheese evenly among tart shells.

Beat egg until frothy. Mix in milk, salt and onion salt. Spoon into shells. Bake in 350°F (180°C) oven for about 20 to 25 minutes until set. Makes 24.

BABY SWISS TARTS: Use grated Swiss cheese instead of Cheddar. May be baked in pie plate to be used as an appetizer.

SPINACH DIP

Served in a crusty bread shell, this makes a spectacular splash, although even served in a bowl, it will still vanish.

Frozen chopped spinach, thawed, drained and blotted dry	10 oz.	284 g
Sour cream	1 cup	250 mL
Mayonnaise	1 cup	250 mL
Chopped green onions	½ cup	125 mL
Parsley flakes	1 tsp.	5 mL
Lemon juice	1 tsp.	5 mL
Seasoned salt	½ tsp.	2 mL
Round crusty bread loaf	1	1

(continued on next page)

Put spinach, sour cream and mayonnaise into bowl. Stir. Add onion, parsley, lemon juice and seasoned salt. Mix together. Chill. Heat before serving.

Cut top from round or oblong loaf. Remove bread from the inside leaving shell about 1 inch (2.5 cm) thick. Reserve removed bread for dipping. Fill with dip. You may need to double the recipe if the loaf is large. Wrap in foil. Heat in 300°F (150°C) oven for 2 hours. Remove from oven and turn foil back. Use reserved bread, cut into pieces, for dipping. After dip is finished break off pieces of shell and enjoy the best part of all.

SAUSAGE ROLLS

A bit fussy to make but when you see how much everyone enjoys them it will all be worthwhile.

Skinless sausages, about 16 to a pound, (450 g) or sausage meat	**16**	**16**
Pie crust or puff pastry, your own or a mix, see page 122		

Fry sausages slowly to remove fat and also to cook. Drain well and cool. This can be done a day ahead. Sausage meat can be used by forming into sausage-shaped rolls with hands dipped in cold water to help keep from sticking. Fry as for sausages. Cool thoroughly.

Roll out pastry on floured surface. Lay a sausage on outer edge. Trim edge evenly. Cut strip the width of sausage. Roll sausage up in pastry, allow extra for overlap, and cut pastry. Dampen overlap to seal. Cut wrapped sausage in half and place on baking tray, sealed side down. Repeat with remaining sausages. When cut in half you have a 2 bite size piece. They may be left whole if a larger snack is desired. Place on ungreased baking tray. Bake in 400°F (200°C) oven for about 20 minutes until browned. Cool. Store in container in refrigerator. Makes 32.

To serve: Arrange on baking tray. Heat in 400°F (200°C) oven for about 10 minutes until hot. May be heated in microwave although crust won't be quite as crisp.

TOURTIÈRE TARTS

Have a supply of these lightly spiced meat tarts in the freezer to heat on demand. Scrumptious.

Ground beef	1 lb.	500 g
Ground pork	½ lb.	225 g
Small onion, finely chopped	1	1
Salt	¾ tsp.	5 mL
Pepper	¼ tsp.	1 mL
Allspice	¼ tsp.	1 mL
Nutmeg	¼ tsp.	1 mL
Garlic powder	¼ tsp.	1 mL
Water	¾ cup	175 mL
Mashed potato	½ cup	125 mL

Pie crust pastry, your own or a mix, see page 122

Put first 9 ingredients into large saucepan. Bring to boil. Stir occasionally as it simmers about 15 minutes.

Add mashed potato. Mixture should be moist and thick. Allow to cool completely.

Line tart tins or muffin tins with pastry. Spoon in meat mixture to fill. Moisten edge and cover with small pastry circle cut to fit. Press to seal. Cut 2 or 3 slits in top. Bake in 400°F (200°C) oven until browned.

Variation: This filling may be used to make turnovers and covered rounds also.

SWEET AND SOUR WINGS

Destined to be the highlight of any party.

Chicken wings	3 lbs.	1.5 kg
Salt and pepper, sprinkle		
Brown sugar, packed	1 cup	250 mL
All-purpose flour	¼ cup	50 mL
Water	½ cup	125 mL
Vinegar	¼ cup	50 mL
Soy sauce	¼ cup	50 mL
Ketchup	1 tbsp.	15 mL

(continued on next page)

Cut off wing tips and discard. Cut wings apart at joint. Place on foil lined baking sheet with sides. Sprinkle salt and pepper on top. Bake in 350°F (180°C) oven for 30 minutes.

Put sugar and flour into saucepan. Stir thoroughly. Add water, vinegar, soy sauce and ketchup. Stir and cook over medium heat until mixture boils and thickens. Remove from heat. When wings have baked for 30 minutes, brush liberally with sauce. Bake 10 minutes more. Brush with sauce again and bake 10 minutes more. If chicken is tender, remove from oven. If not, brush with sauce once more and continue to bake until done. Serve hot. Makes about 36 pieces.

SHRIMP COCKTAIL

A family favorite to begin a favorite family meal.

Crisp lettuce, shredded	1½ cups	375 mL
Medium shrimp, rinsed and drained	4 oz.	113 g
Chili sauce	¾ cup	150 mL
Lemon juice	2 tsp.	10 mL
Worcestershire sauce	¼ - 1 tsp.	1 - 5 mL
Onion powder	½ tsp.	2 mL
Salt	¼ tsp.	1 mL
Peeled and diced apple	½ cup	125 mL
Finely chopped celery	¼ cup	50 mL

Line sherbet glasses with lettuce. Divide shrimp among sherbets, saving a few for garnish if desired.

Mix remaining ingredients in bowl, using smallest amount of Worchestershire sauce. Add until the right amount for you is reached. Spoon over shrimp shortly before serving. Serve with 2 small crackers placed beside each cocktail (Ritz is good). Makes 4 to 5 servings.

Variation: Omit apple. Double amount of celery.

SHRIMP DIP

Any chip would love to be dipped into this.

Cream cheese, softened	8 oz.	250 g
Mayonnaise	¼ cup	50 mL
Chili sauce	2 tsp.	10 mL
Lemon juice	1 tsp.	5 mL
Worcestershire sauce	1 tsp.	5 mL
Dill weed	¼ tsp.	1 mL
Garlic powder, to taste		
Small or broken shrimp, rinsed and drained	4 oz.	113 g

Mash cream cheese with mayonnaise and chili sauce. Add lemon juice, Worcestershire sauce, dill and garlic. Mix well.

Add shrimp. Continue to mash and mix together until of dipping consistency. Makes 2 cups. (500 mL).

BEST CHEESE BALL

When someone has the courage to cut into this beauty, it will quickly be sampled by everyone.

Cream cheese, room temperature	2 x 8 oz.	2 x 250 g
Shredded sharp Cheddar cheese	2 cups	500 mL
Worcestershire sauce	2 tsp.	10 mL
Onion flakes	1 tsp.	5 mL
Lemon juice	1 tsp.	5 mL
Cayenne pepper	⅛ tsp.	0.5 mL
Salt	⅛ tsp.	0.5 mL
Pecans or walnuts, finely chopped		

Measure first 7 ingredients into bowl. Mash and mix together. Shape into ball.

Roll in nuts. Put cocktail knives and crackers nearby so guests can dig right in. Leftovers may be reshaped, rewrapped and frozen if not going to be used within a week. Makes about 3¼ cups (875 mL).

Variation: Add 1 tbsp. (15 mL) chopped green pepper and 1 tbsp. (15 mL) chopped pimiento. Tiny balls are attractive.

SAVORY ONION BREAD

Looks great. Tastes great. Goes well with green salads.

All-purpose flour	1½ cups	375 mL
Baking powder	3 tsp.	15 mL
Salt	1 tsp.	5 mL
Cold butter or margarine	2 tbsp.	30 mL
Grated sharp Cheddar cheese	½ cup	125 mL
Finely chopped onion	½ cup	125 mL
Butter or margarine	1 tbsp.	15 mL
Egg, slightly beaten	1	1
Milk	½ cup	125 mL
Grated sharp Cheddar cheese	½ cup	125 mL

Combine flour, baking powder and salt in large bowl. Cut in first amount of butter until crumbly. Stir in cheese. Make a well in center.

Fry onion slowly in remaining butter until clear and golden. Set aside.

Beat egg with spoon in small bowl. Stir in milk. Add onion. Pour into well. Stir to moisten and form a soft dough. Pat into greased 8 inch (20 cm) round or square pan.

Sprinkle cheese over top. Bake in 400° F (200° C) oven for 25 minutes. Serve hot to 6 medium appetites.

CINNAMON TOAST

A Sunday night tradition with our family.

Butter or margarine, softened	1 cup	250 mL
Brown sugar, packed	2½ cups	625 mL
Cinnamon	2½ tbsp.	40 mL

Have butter soft. Mix all together well until spreadable. Resist the urge to add more butter. It would be easier to spread but makes the flavor too bland. Store in covered container in refrigerator if you used butter, on kitchen shelf if you used margarine.

Spread on hot toast as desired.

SCOTTISH OAT SCONES

Nibble or lunch on it. It won't last for long.

All-purpose flour	1½ cups	375 mL
Rolled oats	2 cups	500 mL
Granulated sugar	¼ cup	50 mL
Baking powder	4 tsp.	20 mL
Salt	½ tsp.	2 mL
Currants	½ cup	125 mL
Egg, beaten	1	1
Butter or margarine, softened	½ cup	125 mL
Milk	⅓ cup	75 mL

Put first six dry ingredients into large bowl. Mix. Make a well in center.

Beat egg until frothy. Mix in melted butter and milk. Pour into well. Stir to make soft dough. Pat into two 6 to 7 inch (15 to 18 cm) circles. Transfer to greased baking sheet. Score each top into 8 pie shaped wedges. Bake in 425° F (220° C) oven for 15 minutes until risen and browned. Split and butter. Yield: 16 scones.

1. Blueberry Pancakes with Maple Syrup page 39
2. Orange Julius page 9
3. Biscuit Melt page 38
4. Pineapple Muffins page 49
5. Corn Muffins page 44
6. Banana Bran Muffins page 38
7. Oatmeal Muffins page 43
8. Jiffy Cinnamon Rolls page 37

Something so easy shouldn't be so good. A single recipe won't be enough.

All-purpose flour	2 cups	500 mL
Granulated sugar	2 tbsp.	30 mL
Baking powder	4 tsp.	20 mL
Salt	1 tsp.	5 mL
Cold butter or margarine	¼ cup	50 mL
Cold milk	1 cup	250 mL
Butter or margarine, softened	⅓ cup	75 mL
Brown sugar, packed	1 cup	250 mL
Cinnamon	3 tsp.	15 mL
Currants or cut up raisins	⅓ cup	75 mL

In large bowl put flour, sugar, baking powder and salt. Cut in first amount of butter until crumbly. Make a well in center.

Pour milk into well. Stir to form soft dough adding a bit more milk if needed. Turn out on lightly floured surface. Knead 8 to 10 times. Roll into rectangle about ⅓ inch (1 cm) thick and 12 inches (30 cm) long.

Cream second amount of butter, brown sugar and cinnamon together well. Drop 1 measuring teaspoon (5 mL) into each of 12 greased muffin tins. Spread the remaining cinnamon mixture over dough rectangle. Sprinkle currants over top. Roll up as for jelly roll. Mark first then cut into 12 slices. Place cut side down in muffin pan. Bake in 400° F (200° C) oven for 20 to 25 minutes. Turn out on tray. Makes 12.

GLAZE: To ½ cup (125 mL) icing sugar, add enough milk or water to make a thin glaze. Drizzle over cinnamon rolls.

Pictured on page 35.

Paré Pointer

He used to feel sorry for a giraffe with a sore throat until he saw a turtle with claustrophobia.

BANANA BRAN MUFFINS

Delicious with a hint of chocolate. Dark and devious! The best.

All-purpose flour	1 cup	250 mL
All bran cereal	1 cup	250 mL
Baking powder	1 tsp.	5 mL
Baking soda	1 tsp.	5 mL
Salt	½ tsp.	2 mL
Cocoa	2 tbsp.	30 mL
Butter or margarine, softened	¼ cup	50 mL
Granulated sugar	½ cup	125 mL
Eggs	2	2
Sour milk (1 tsp., 5 mL, vinegar in milk)	¼ cup	50 mL
Mashed bananas (3 medium)	1 cup	250 mL

Measure all six dry ingredients into mixing bowl. Stir to combine. Make a well in center.

Cream butter, sugar and one egg until well blended. Beat in second egg. Mix in sour milk and bananas. Pour all at once into well. Mix until moistened. Ignore lumps. Fill greased muffin tins ¾ full. Bake in 400°F (200°C) oven for 20 to 25 minutes. Yield: 12 muffins.

Pictured on page 35.

BISCUIT MELT

A cheese mixture melted over biscuits. You will most likely need to double the recipe.

Refrigerated biscuits - pkg. of 10	1	1
Egg	1	1
Cream	2 tbsp.	30 mL
Dry mustard powder	⅛ tsp.	0.5 mL
Salt	¼ tsp.	1 mL
Grated Cheddar cheese	⅔ cup	150 mL

Arrange biscuits in an ungreased 8 inch (20 cm) pie plate.

Mix remaining ingredients together. Spoon over top. Bake in 425°F (220°C) oven for about 10 minutes. Serve hot. Makes 10.

Note: This works very well with baking powder biscuits.

Pictured on page 35.

PANCAKES

So easy to whip up from scratch. Can be increased quickly for extra plates.

All-purpose flour	1½ cups	375 mL
Granulated sugar	1 tbsp.	15 mL
Baking powder	1 tbsp.	15 mL
Salt	½ tsp.	2 mL
Egg, beaten	1	1
Cooking oil	2 tbsp.	30 mL
Milk	1½ cups	375 mL

Combine flour, sugar, baking powder and salt in medium size bowl.

Beat egg slightly in small bowl. Mix in oil and milk. Add to dry ingredients. Stir. A few small lumps in batter are preferable. Add more or less milk to have thicker or thinner pancakes. Pan is ready when drops of water bounce all over it. Drop batter by spoonfuls onto lightly greased hot pan 380°F (190°C). When bubbles appear and edges begin to dry, turn to brown other side. Serve hot with butter and maple syrup. Makes 12.

GRAHAM PANCAKES: Use 1¼ cups (300 mL) flour and add ½ cup (125 mL) graham cracker crumbs.

BLUEBERRY PANCAKES: Fold in ¾ to 1 cup (175 to 250 mL) blueberries.

Pictured on page 35.

WHEAT GERM PANCAKES: Add ½ cup (125 mL) wheat germ plus ¼ cup (50 mL) more milk to batter.

MAPLE SYRUP

Make your own. It's so easy and fast.

Brown sugar, packed	2 cups	500 mL
Water	1 cup	250 mL
Maple flavoring	1 tsp.	5 mL

In medium saucepan combine sugar and water. Bring to a boil stirring frequently. Remove from heat and add flavoring. Serve with pancakes, waffles and French toast. Makes 2 cups.

Pictured on page 35.

BEST CHEESE BISCUITS

These taste as good as they look.

All-purpose flour	2 cups	500 mL
Baking powder	4 tsp.	20 mL
Granulated sugar	2 tbsp.	30 mL
Salt	¾ tsp.	5 mL
Grated sharp Cheddar cheese	1 cup	250 mL
Cooking oil	⅓ cup	75 mL
Milk	¾ cup	175 mL

Measure first 4 dry ingredients together in bowl. Add grated cheese. Stir.

Add cooking oil and milk. Stir to form a soft ball of dough. Add more milk if needed to make dough soft. Turn out on lightly floured board and knead gently 8 to 10 times. Roll or pat to ¾ to 1 inch (2 to 2.5 cm) thick. Cut with biscuit cutter. Place on ungreased cookie sheet close together for moist sides or one inch (2 cm) apart for crisp sides. Dab tops with milk for nicer browning. Bake in 425° F (220° C) oven for 15 minutes until nicely browned. Serve plain or with butter. Makes 1 dozen.

Note: Medium cheese can be used but it doesn't give as much flavor.

Pictured on page 215.

CRANBERRY BISCUITS: Omit cheese. Add 1 cup (250 mL) chopped cranberries, fresh or frozen. Pretty and tasty.

RICH TEA BISCUITS

Quick to make for a meal or a lunch.

All-purpose flour	2 cups	500 mL
Granulated sugar	2 tbsp.	30 mL
Salt	1 tsp.	5 mL
Baking powder	4 tsp.	20 mL
Cream of tartar	½ tsp.	2 mL
Butter or margarine, cold	½ cup	125 mL
Cold milk	¾ cup	200 mL

(continued on next page)

Put first 5 ingredients into bowl. Stir thoroughly.

Cut in butter until crumbly.

Pour in milk. Stir quickly to combine. Dough should be soft. Add a bit more milk if needed. Turn out on lightly floured surface. Knead gently 8 to 10 times. Roll or pat ½ to ¾ inch (2 cm) thick or half the thickness you want the baked product to be. Cut with small round cookie cutter. Place on greased cookie sheet close together for soft sides or apart for crisp sides. Bake in 450° F (230° C) oven for 12 to 15 minutes. Brushing biscuits with milk before baking will produce a pretty brown top. Makes 10.

Pictured on page 161.

CHEESE LOAF

Moist, delicious and attractive. A good bread substitute. And so simple to make.

All-purpose flour	3 cups	750 mL
Baking powder	4 tsp.	20 mL
Salt	½ tsp.	3 mL
Grated medium or sharp cheese	1½ cups	375 mL
Milk	1½ cups	375 mL
Butter or margarine, melted	2 tbsp.	30 mL

Combine flour, baking powder, salt and cheese in large bowl. Stir thoroughly.

Add milk and melted butter. Stir to form soft dough. Put in greased loaf pan 9 x 5 x 3 inch (23 x 12 x 7 cm). Bake in 400° F (200° C) oven for 35 to 40 minutes. Remove from pan to cool. Serve with butter. Yield: 1 loaf.

Paré Pointer

The mother ghost took her little ghost to the doctor to find out why he was in such good spirits.

CURRENT SCONES

Just right for a morning coffee party.

All-purpose flour	2 cups	450 mL
Granulated sugar	¼ cup	50 mL
Baking powder	4 tsp.	20 mL
Salt	½ tsp.	2 mL
Cold butter or margarine	¼ cup	50 mL
Currants	½ cup	125 mL
Egg	1	1
Milk	⅔ cup	150 mL

Milk for brushing tops
Granulated sugar for sprinkling

In a large bowl put flour, sugar, baking powder and salt. Add butter. Cut in until crumbly. Stir in currants. Make a well in center.

In small bowl, beat egg until frothy. Stir in milk. Pour into well. Stir with a fork to form soft dough. Turn out on lightly floured surface. Knead 8 to 10 times. Divide into two equal parts. Pat each into 6 inch (15 cm) circle. Transfer to greased baking sheet. Brush tops with milk and sprinkle with sugar. Score each top into 6 pie shaped markings. Bake in 425° F (220° C) oven for 15 minutes until risen and browned slightly. Serve hot with butter and jam. Yield: 12 scones.

Paré Pointer

Scientists seem to be looking for the same things. They always re-search everything.

OATMEAL MUFFINS

Try your oatmeal in a muffin instead of a bowl. These are excellent with or without the addition of coconut or dates.

Rolled oats	1 cup	250 mL
Buttermilk	1 cup	250 mL
All-purpose flour	1 cup	250 mL
Brown sugar, packed	¾ cup	175 mL
Baking powder	1 tsp.	5 mL
Baking soda	½ tsp.	2 mL
Salt	¼ tsp.	1 mL
Egg	1	1
Butter or margarine, melted	¼ cup	60 mL
Coconut or chopped dates (optional)	¼ cup	60 mL

Put rolled oats and buttermilk into small bowl. Stir until moistened throughout. Let stand.

In larger bowl measure in flour, sugar, baking powder, baking soda and salt. Stir together to mix. Make a well in center.

Add egg and melted butter to oat mixture. Mix well. Pour all at once into well. Stir to moisten.

These muffins are good without additions or you may add coconut or dates. Fill greased muffin tins ¾ full. Bake in 400°F (200°C) oven for about 20 minutes until an inserted toothpick comes out clean. Makes 1 dozen.

Pictured on page 35.

Paré Pointer

It isn't hard to spot a leopard. They come that way.

APPLE STREUSEL MUFFINS

This fancy muffin is the "icing on the cake". Good.

TOPPING

Brown sugar, packed	½ cup	125 mL
All-purpose flour	¼ cup	50 mL
Butter or margarine, softened	¼ cup	50 mL

In small bowl rub sugar, flour and butter until crumbly. Set aside.

All-purpose flour	1½ cups	375 mL
Granulated sugar	½ cup	125 mL
Baking powder	3 tsp.	15 mL
Salt	½ tsp.	2 mL
Egg	1	1
Milk	¼ cup	60 mL
Cooking oil	¼ cup	60 mL
Shredded apple, peeled or not	¾ cup	175 mL

In mixing bowl stir flour, sugar, baking powder and salt together. Make a well in center.

In another bowl beat egg, milk and oil to blend. Stir in apple. Pour into well. Stir until just moistened. Fill muffin tins ¾ full. Sprinkle with topping. Bake in 400°F (200°C) oven for 20 to 25 minutes. Makes 12.

CORN MUFFINS

Not only different, but excellent as well. Contains sour cream.

All-purpose flour	1 cup	250 mL
Yellow cornmeal	1 cup	250 mL
Granulated sugar	¼ cup	50 mL
Baking powder	1 tsp.	5 mL
Baking soda	1 tsp.	5 mL
Salt	1 tsp.	5 mL
Eggs	2	2
Sour cream	1 cup	250 mL
Butter or margarine, melted	¼ cup	60 mL

(continued on next page)

Measure first 6 ingredients into bowl. Stir together. Make a well in center.

In another bowl beat eggs and sour cream. Add melted butter and mix. Pour into well. Stir just enough to moisten. Fill greased muffin cups ¾ full. Bake in 425°F (220°C) oven for about 15 to 20 minutes. Let stand 5 minutes then remove. Makes 12 muffins.

Pictured on page 35.

BRAN MUFFINS

Can easily be doubled for freezing. Top notch. Gail's favorite.

All-purpose flour	1 cup	250 mL
Baking powder	1 tsp.	5 mL
Baking soda	1 tsp.	5 mL
Salt	½ tsp.	2 mL
Raisins	¾ cup	175 mL
Buttermilk or sour milk	1 cup	250 mL
Natural bran	1 cup	250 mL
Cooking oil	⅓ cup	75 mL
Molasses	3 tbsp.	50 mL
Egg	1	1
Brown sugar, packed	¼ cup	50 mL
Vanilla	½ tsp.	2 mL

In large bowl put flour, baking powder, soda, salt and raisins. Stir together well. Push up around sides of bowl making well in center.

In another bowl stir buttermilk with bran. Let stand 5 minutes.

Add remaining ingredients to bran mixture in order given. Beat with spoon until mixed. Pour into well in first bowl. Stir just to moisten. Batter will be lumpy. Fill greased muffin tins ¾ full. Bake in 375°F (190°C) oven for 20 to 25 minutes. Let stand 5 minutes. Remove from pan. Makes 12.

STREUSEL COFFEE CAKE

A good reliable stand-by. Easy to make for company "on the way"

Butter or margarine, softened	⅓ cup	75 mL
Granulated sugar	½ cup	125 mL
Egg	1	1
All-purpose flour	1½ cups	350 mL
Baking powder	2 tsp.	10 mL
Salt	½ tsp.	2 mL
Milk	¾ cup	175 mL
TOPPING		
Brown sugar, packed	½ cup	125 mL
All-purpose flour	2 tbsp.	30 mL
Cinnamon	1 tsp.	5 mL
Butter or margarine, melted	3 tbsp.	50 mL

Cream butter, sugar and egg together well in mixing bowl.

Stir flour, baking powder and salt together.

Measure out milk. Add alternately with flour mixture. Scrape into greased 9 x 9 inch (22 x 22 cm) pan. Smooth top.

Topping: Mix brown sugar, flour, cinnamon and melted butter together. Using fingers for easy distribution, sprinkle over batter. Bake in 375° F (190° C) oven for about 35 minutes until an inserted toothpick comes out clean. Serve warm.

APPLE COFFEE CAKE

So quick and easy to make. Has a crunchy topping

Yellow cake mix, 2 layer size	1	1
Canned apple pie filling	19 oz.	540 mL
Eggs	3	3
Cinnamon	½ tsp.	2 mL
Butter or margarine, softened	½ cup	125 mL
Granulated sugar	½ cup	125 mL
All-purpose flour	1 cup	250 mL

(continued on next page)

Put cake mix, apple pie filling, eggs and cinnamon into mixing bowl. Stir together. Turn into greased 9 x 13 inch (22 x 33 cm) pan.

Mix butter, sugar and flour together until crumbly. Sprinkle over top. Bake in 350° F (180° C) oven for about 50 minutes or until it tests done with toothpick. Serve warm or cool. Cuts into 15 generous pieces.

ORANGE MUFFINS

A delicious orange flavor with little date flecks throughout. Scrumptious!

Orange with peel, cut up	1	1
Orange juice	½ cup	125 mL
Chopped dates	½ cup	125 mL
Egg	1	1
Butter or margarine	½ cup	125 mL
All-purpose flour	1¾ cups	425 mL
Granulated sugar	¾ cup	175 mL
Baking powder	1 tsp.	5 mL
Baking soda	1 tsp.	5 mL

Cut orange into 7 or 8 pieces. Remove seeds. Combine orange pieces and juice in blender. Purée.

Add dates, egg and butter to blender. Blend. Pour into medium size bowl.

Measure flour, sugar, baking powder and soda in separate bowl. Mix thoroughly. Pour over top of orange mixture. Stir to combine. Fill greased muffin tins ¾ full. Bake in 400° F (200° C) oven for 20 minutes. Remove from pans after 5 minutes standing time. Makes 12 large or 16 medium muffins.

Paré Pointer

Don't ever do arithmetic near a tiger. If you add four and four you might get ate.

SOUR CREAM COFFEE CAKE

A favorite cinnamony coffee cake.

Butter or margarine, softened	½ cup	125 mL
Granulated sugar	1 cup	250 mL
Eggs	2	2
Baking soda	1 tsp.	5 mL
Sour cream	1 cup	250 mL
All-purpose flour	1½ cups	375 mL
Baking powder	1½ tsp.	7 mL
Salt	¼ tsp.	1 mL
Brown sugar, packed	½ cup	125 mL
Cinnamon	1 tsp.	5 mL
Finely chopped nuts	½ cup	125 mL

Cream butter, sugar and 1 egg together well in mixing bowl. Beat in second egg. Add soda and sour cream. Mix.

Mix flour, baking powder and salt together. Add to batter. Stir to mix. Put one half batter in greased 9 x 9 inch (22 x 22 cm) pan.

Mix brown sugar, cinnamon and nuts together. Sprinkle one half over batter. Spoon second half of batter here and there over top. Sprinkle second half of cinnamon mixture over all. Bake in 350°F (180°C) oven for 45 minutes or until an inserted toothpick comes out clean. Serve warm with or without Creamy Rum Sauce, below.

Pictured on page 53.

CREAMY RUM SAUCE

A rich creamy colored sauce. This has such a fantastic flavor you will need to make lots.

Granulated sugar	1 cup	250 mL
All-purpose flour	2 tbsp.	30 mL
Salt	¼ tsp.	1 mL
Light cream	1 cup	250 mL
Vanilla	1 tsp.	5 mL
Rum flavoring	1 tsp.	5 mL
Butter or margarine	2 tbsp.	30 mL

(continued on next page)

Stir sugar, flour and salt together well in small saucepan.

Add cream, vanilla, rum flavoring and butter. Mix. Heat and stir until it boils and thickens. Serve over coffee cake, steamed pudding or plain cake. Makes 1⅓ cups (300 mL).

Pictured on page 53.

PINEAPPLE MUFFINS

Moist and tender with a good pineapple flavor.

Cream cheese, softened	4 oz.	125 g
Granulated sugar	1 cup	250 mL
Egg	1	1
Vanilla	1 tsp.	5 mL
Sour cream	½ cup	125 mL
Crushed pineapple, drained	19 oz.	540 mL
All-purpose flour	2 cups	500 mL
Baking soda	1 tsp.	5 mL
Salt	1 tsp.	5 mL

Beat cheese and sugar together. Beat in egg and vanilla. Add sour cream. Mix. Stir in pineapple.

Stir flour, baking soda and salt together and add. Mix only until moistened. Fill greased muffin cups ¾ full. Bake in 350°F (180°C) oven for about 30 minutes. Let stand about 5 minutes before removing from pan. Makes 16 medium muffins.

Pictured on page 35.

Pare Pointer

The dog ate the frankfurter in a bun. It's a dog-eat-dog world out there.

DATE LOAF

Extra moist, extra yummy.

Dates, cut up	1¼ cups	300 mL
Boiling water	¾ cup	175 mL
Baking soda	1 tsp.	5 mL
Egg	1	1
Brown sugar, packed	¾ cup	175 mL
Salt	¾ tsp.	3 mL
Vanilla	1 tsp.	5 mL
All-purpose flour	1½ cups	375 mL
Baking powder	1 tsp.	5 mL
Chopped walnuts	½ cup	125 mL
Butter or margarine, melted	¼ cup	50 mL

In small bowl put cut up dates, boiling water and soda. Stir and cool.

Beat egg lightly. Add sugar, salt and vanilla. Beat to mix. Stir in date mixture.

Mix flour and baking powder together then pour into date mixture. Stir to mix. Stir in nuts and melted butter. Pour into greased 9 x 5 x 3 inch (23 x 12 x 7 cm) loaf pan. Let stand for 20 minutes, then bake in 350°F (180°C) oven for 1 hour. Let stand for 10 minutes. Remove from pan. Cool and wrap. Yield: 1 loaf.

Pictured on page 53.

TOFFEE LOAF

Sweetened condensed milk gives this favorite loaf its distinctive toffee flavor.

Raisins	1½ cups	375 mL
Chopped dates	1¼ cup	300 mL
Currants	½ cup	125 mL
Butter or margarine	1 cup	250 mL
Water	½ cup	125 mL
Condensed milk (not evaporated)	11 oz.	300 mL
All-purpose flour	2 cups	500 mL
Baking soda	1 tsp.	5 mL
Baking powder	1 tsp.	5 mL
Salt	¼ tsp.	2 mL

(continued on next page)

Place all three fruits in large, heavy saucepan. Stir in butter, water and condensed milk. Bring to a boil over medium heat and simmer for 3 minutes stirring frequently. Time accurately. Remove from heat. Pour into large mixing bowl to cool for 30 minutes.

Meanwhile, stir in flour, soda, baking powder and salt together in small bowl. When 30 minutes are up, stir in fruit mixture. Spoon into greased 9 x 5 x 3 inch (23 x 12 x 7 cm) loaf pan. Bake in 325° F (160° C) oven for about 1½ hours. About halfway through baking lay a piece of aluminum foil over top if you feel it is getting too brown. Loaf should show signs of shrinking away from edges of pan. Cool in pan 15 minutes, then remove to rack to finish cooling. Store in plastic bag. Yield: 1 loaf.

Pictured on page 53.

LEMON RAISIN LOAF

A large, moist loaf and really good! A must to try.

Boiling water	1 cup	250 mL
Raisins	1½ cups	375 mL
Baking soda	1 tsp.	5 mL
Butter or margarine, softened	½ cup	125 mL
Brown sugar, packed	1¼ cups	300 mL
Egg	1	1
Grated rind of lemon	1	1
Juice of lemon	1	1
All-purpose flour	2½ cups	625 mL
Baking powder	1 tsp.	5 mL
Salt	½ tsp.	2 mL
Chopped nuts	½ cup	125 mL

Pour water over raisins and baking soda in saucepan. Bring to boil. Remove from heat. Cool.

Beat butter, sugar and egg together well. Stir in lemon rind, juice and cooled raisin mixture.

In another bowl stir together flour, baking powder, salt and chopped nuts. Add all at once into batter, stirring until combined. Pour into greased loaf pan 9 x 5 x 3 inch (23 x 12 x 7 cm). Bake for about 1 hour in 350° F (180° C) oven. Test with toothpick. Let stand for 10 minutes before removing from pan to cool on rack. Wrap. It cuts better the next day. Yield: 1 loaf.

Pictured on page 53.

BANANA BREAD

An old stand-by. Quite dark with lots of flecks.

Butter or margarine, softened	½ cup	125 mL
Granulated sugar	1 cup	250 mL
Eggs	2	2
Mashed very ripe bananas (3 medium)	1 cup	250 mL
All-purpose flour	1¾ cups	425 mL
Baking soda	1 tsp.	5 mL
Baking powder	½ tsp.	2 mL
Salt	½ tsp.	2 mL
Chopped walnuts	1 cup	250 mL

Cream butter and sugar together. Beat in eggs one at a time, beating until smooth. Add mashed bananas and blend in.

In second bowl, stir flour with baking soda, baking powder, salt and nuts. Add to banana mixture stirring only to moisten. Transfer to greased 9 x 5 x 3 inch (23 x 12 x 7 cm) loaf pan. Bake in 350°F (180°C) oven for about 1 hour until inserted toothpick comes out clean. Let stand 10 minutes. Remove from pan and place on cake rack to cool. Wrap to store. Yield: 1 loaf.

BANANA CHIP BREAD: Add ¾ cup (175 mL) semisweet chocolate chips.

A quick way to make this ring rather than the usual yeast dough. Almost too pretty to eat.

FILLING

Cream cheese, softened	8 oz.	250 g
Granulated sugar	¼ cup	50 mL
Vanilla	½ tsp.	2 mL

BREAD

All-purpose flour	2 cups	500 mL
Granulated sugar	2 tbsp.	30 mL
Baking powder	4 tsp.	20 mL
Salt	¾ tsp.	4 mL
Cold butter or margarine	¼ cup	60 mL
Cold milk	1 cup	250 mL

Nuts, raisins, chopped cherries

Filling: Beat cheese, first amount of sugar and vanilla in small bowl until smooth. Set aside.

Bread: Combine flour, second amount of sugar, baking powder and salt in bowl. Cut in butter until crumbly.

Add ¾ cup (175 mL) of milk first, adding the remaining ¼ cup (75 mL) if necessary to make soft dough. Roll on lightly floured surface into rectangle, about 8 x 12 inches (20 x 30 cm). Spread with cheese mixture. Sprinkle with nuts, raisins and chopped cherries. Beginning at long side, roll up into roll. Seal edge. Place on greased baking sheet, shaping into a circle. Seal ends together. Using scissors, cut over halfway through roll every inch (2.5 cm). Turn each cut section on its side. Bake in 425°F (220°C) oven for about 15 to 20 minutes until browned. Brush with corn syrup to glaze while hot. May also be glazed with white icing. Add enough water to ½ cup (125 mL) icing (confectioner's) sugar to make a barely pourable glaze. Drizzle over cooled tea ring.

Pictured on page 53.

Paré Pointer

When the judge threw the book at him, he read it and smartened up.

TEA BREAD

A fine textured loaf with a delicate flavor. Perfect for tea.

Butter, softened	½ cup	125 mL
Granulated sugar	1 cup	250 mL
Eggs	2	2
Vanilla	1 tsp.	5 mL
All-purpose flour	2 cups	500 mL
Baking powder	1 tsp.	5 mL
Milk	1 cup	250 mL

Cream butter and sugar together. Beat in eggs and vanilla.

Stir flour and baking powder together. Add flour mixture alternately with milk.

Pour into greased 9 x 5 inch (23 x 12 cm) loaf pan. Bake in 350° F (180° C) oven for about 1 hour or until an inserted toothpick comes out clean. Makes 1 loaf.

Pictured on page 53.

LUXURY LOAF

A different loaf absolutely filled with flecks of chocolate.

Butter or margarine, softened	1 cup	225 mL
Granulated sugar	1 cup	225 mL
Eggs	5	5
Vanilla	1 tsp.	5 mL
Grated rind of orange	1	1
Orange juice	¼ cup	50 mL
All-purpose flour	2 cups	450 mL
Baking powder	1 tsp.	5 mL
Salt	½ tsp.	2 mL
Nutmeg	¼ tsp.	2 mL
Grated semisweet chocolate	4 oz.	113 g
Chopped nuts	⅓ cup	75 mL

(continued on next page)

Cream butter and sugar together well until fluffy. Beat in eggs one at a time, beating well after each addition. Stir in vanilla, rind and juice.

Put flour, baking powder, salt and nutmeg into another bowl. Stir in grated chocolate and nuts. Pour into first bowl. Stir all together until moistened. Spoon into greased loaf pan 9 x 5 x 3 inch (23 x 12 x 7 cm). Bake in 325°F (170°C) oven for 1 hour and 15 minutes until a toothpick inserted in center comes out clean. Let stand 10 minutes. Remove loaf from pan to cool on cake rack. Wrap. Yield: 1 loaf.

Pictured on page 53.

CHOCOLATE CHIP DATE LOAF

Dark and delicious with fine texture. A large loaf. Good!

Chopped dates	1 cup	250 mL
Baking soda	1 tsp.	5 mL
Boiling water	1 cup	250 mL
Vanilla	1 tsp.	5 mL
Butter or margarine, softened	¾ cup	175 mL
Granulated sugar	1 cup	250 mL
Eggs	2	2
All-purpose flour	2 cups	500 mL
Cocoa	½ cup	125 mL
Baking soda	1 tsp.	5 mL
Salt	½ tsp.	2 mL
Semisweet chocolate chips	½ cup	125 mL

In a small bowl combine dates, soda, boiling water and vanilla. Stir. Set aside to cool a little.

In mixing bowl cream butter and sugar. Beat eggs in one at a time, beating until smooth. Add date mixture. Stir.

Measure flour, cocoa, soda, salt and chips into a separate bowl. Stir to mix well then pour flour mixture into mixing bowl. Blend until just moistened. Spoon into greased 9 x 5 x 3 inch (23 x 12 x 7 cm) loaf pan. Bake for 1 hour in 350°F (180°C) oven or until it tests done with toothpick. Wait about 10 minutes for loaf to cool a bit before removing it to a rack to finish cooling. Wrap. Yield: 1 loaf.

APPLE LOAF

A good moist loaf with mild cinnamon and apple flavor.

Eggs	2	2
Granulated sugar	1 cup	250 mL
Cooking oil	½ cup	125 mL
Vanilla	½ tsp.	2 mL
Grated peeled apple	2 cups	500 mL
All-purpose flour	2 cups	500 mL
Baking soda	1 tsp.	5 mL
Salt	½ tsp.	2 mL
Raisins	1 cup	250 mL
Chopped walnuts	½ cup	125 mL
Granulated sugar	4 tsp.	20 mL
Cinnamon	½ tsp.	2 mL

Beat eggs in mixing bowl until frothy. Beat in first amount of sugar, cooking oil and vanilla. Mix in apple.

Stir flour, baking soda and salt together and add. Mix together. Stir in raisins and walnuts. Scrape into greased 9 x 5 inch (23 x 12 cm) loaf pan.

Stir remaining sugar and cinnamon together. Sprinkle over top. Bake in 350°F (180°C) oven for about 1 hour until it tests done with toothpick. Makes 1 loaf.

RHUBARB BREAD

Orange and rhubarb combine to make a colorful loaf. Tasty.

Finely cut rhubarb	1 cup	250 mL
Granulated sugar	¼ cup	60 mL
Granulated sugar	1 cup	250 mL
Butter or margarine, melted	¼ cup	60 mL
Egg	1	1
Orange, rind and juice	1	1
Milk added to make	1 cup	250 mL
All-purpose flour	3 cups	750 mL
Baking powder	1½ tbsp.	25 mL
Salt	½ tsp.	2 mL

(continued on next page)

58

Combine rhubarb with first amount of sugar. Let stand 15 minutes.

In mixing bowl put remaining sugar, melted butter and egg. Beat well.

Put grated orange rind and orange juice into measuring cup. Add milk to measure 1 cup (250 mL). Stir into batter.

Stir flour, baking powder and salt together and add. Stir until moistened. Turn into greased 9 x 5 inch (23 x 12 cm) loaf pan. Bake in 350°F (180°C) oven for about 1 hour until it tests done with toothpick. Makes 1 loaf.

Pictured on page 53.

LAVOSH

This crisp, nutty flavored flatbread can be served with soup or just as a snack.

Egg, beaten	1	1
Cooking oil	1 tbsp.	15 mL
Milk	⅔ cup	150 mL
All-purpose flour	2 ⅔ cups	600 mL
Salt	1½ tsp.	7 mL
Granulated sugar	2 tsp.	10 mL
Sesame seeds	2 tbsp.	30 mL

Beat egg until frothy. Add remaining ingredients. Mix together well. Dough will be stiff. Let stand 30 minutes. Divide dough into 6 pieces. Roll out very thinly — as thinly as you can and still be able to handle it. Bake on ungreased cooking sheet. Bake on rack in top third part of 375°F (190°C) oven for 15 minutes until browned. Put cake pan containing some water on lower rack for moisture the first five minutes and remove water for the remainder. Break in chunks to store in plastic bag when cool. Sesame seeds may be sprinkled over top of dough during last part of rolling rather than added to dough during mixing if you find it easier. They tend to drop out when dough is being handled. Yield 6 sheets.

Pictured on page 179.

BEEF NOODLE BAKE

Just the dish to go from refrigerator to oven. Excellent choice.

Ground beef	1 lb.	500 g
Condensed tomato soup	10 oz.	284 mL
Condensed cream of mushroom soup	10 oz.	284 mL
Chopped celery	1 cup	250 mL
Chopped onion	1 cup	250 mL
Chow mein noodles	1 cup	250 mL
Soy sauce	2 tbsp.	30 mL

Chow mein noodles

Scramble fry ground beef until browned. Put into 1½ quart (1.5 L) casserole.

Add next 6 ingredients. Stir to mix well. Smooth top.

Sprinkle extra noodles over top. Bake uncovered in 375°F (190°C) oven for 45 minutes or to the degree of doneness you like celery and onion. Serves 4.

Pictured on page 71.

TUNA PIE

A can of tuna done up in high fashion. Freezes well. Doubles as an appetizer also.

Pastry for 2 crusts, your own or a mix, see page 122

Canned tuna, drained	5.2 oz.	147 g
Finely chopped onion	½ cup	125 mL
Finely chopped celery	2 tbsp.	30 mL
Frozen peas	1 cup	250 mL
Shredded carrot	¼ cup	50 mL
Condensed cream of mushroom soup	10 oz.	284 mL
Parsley flakes	1 tsp.	5 mL

Roll crust and fit into 9 inch (22 cm) pie plate.

Mix remaining ingredients together. Spread into pie shell. Roll second crust. Dampen edge of bottom crust, then cover with second crust. Crimp edges to seal. Cut slits in top. Bake in 375°F (190°C) oven until browned, about 45 minutes. Cut into 6 wedges for main meal and into 16 wedges for appetizers.

Pictured on page 71.

LASAGNE

No precooking of noodles. Whether served for a meal or a sumptuous late night snack, this is one of the best freezer foods to have on hand.

Ground beef	1 lb.	500 g
Canned tomatoes	2 x 28 oz.	2 x 796 mL
Tomato sauce	7½ oz.	213 mL
Garlic salt	¼ tsp.	1 mL
Envelope spaghetti sauce mix	1	1
Cottage cheese	1 cup	250 g
Egg	1	1
Grated Parmesan cheese	½ cup	125 mL
Mozzarella cheese, shredded	6 oz.	170 g
Wide lasagne noodles, raw	8 oz.	225 g

Brown beef in frying pan. Break up any lumps.

Add tomatoes, sauce, garlic and spaghetti sauce mix. Bring to boil and simmer slowly for 10 minutes. Put some of this on bottom of 9 x 13 inch (22 x 23 cm) pan — just enough to keep noodles from resting on bottom of pan.

In small mixing bowl mix cottage cheese, egg and Parmesan together well.

Assemble:
1. Bit of meat sauce
2. Layer of raw noodles
3. One-half of meat sauce
4. Cottage cheese mixture
5. Layer of raw noodles
6. One-half of meat sauce
7. Mozzarella cheese

Cover tightly with foil. Grease foil to help prevent cheese from sticking. Bake in 350° F (180° C) oven for 1 hour or more until noodles are tender. Let stand 10 minutes before serving. Serves 8 generous portions or 12 average.

Pictured on page 89.

TOMATO DUMPLINGS

For something different, try this old classic.

Canned tomatoes	28 oz.	796 mL
Granulated sugar	1 tsp.	5 mL
Finely chopped onion	¼ cup	50 mL
Finely chopped celery	2 tbsp.	30 mL
Water	½ cup	125 mL
Salt	½ tsp.	2 mL
All-purpose flour	1 cup	250 mL
Baking powder	2 tsp.	10 mL
Sugar	1 tsp.	5 mL
Salt	½ tsp.	2 mL
Shortening	1 tbsp.	15 mL
Milk	½ cup	125 mL

In large pot combine tomatoes, sugar, onion, celery, water and salt. Bring to boil.

In medium size bowl combine flour, baking powder, sugar and salt. Cut in shortening until crumbly. Add milk. Stir to mix. Drop by spoonfuls over boiling tomatoes. Cover. Keep boiling without removing lid for 15 minutes. Serves 6.

Pictured on back cover.

BEST HASH BROWNS

Prepare this early in the day. Bake when needed. Creamy and convenient.

Condensed cream of celery soup	10 oz.	284 mL
Condensed cream of chicken soup	10 oz.	284 mL
Sour cream	2 cups	500 mL
Onion flakes	3 tbsp.	50 mL
Grated Cheddar cheese	2 cups	500 mL
Seasoned salt	2 tsp.	10 mL
Butter or margarine, melted	½ cup	125 mL
Frozen hash brown potatoes, partly thawed	2 lbs.	900 g
Cornflake crumbs	½ cup	125 mL

(continued on next page)

In large bowl mix first 7 ingredients together.

Add hash browns and stir to mix. Transfer to greased 9 x 13 inch (22 x 33 cm) pan.

Top with cornflake crumbs if you are using them. Bake uncovered in 350°F (180°C) oven for about 1 hour. Serves 10 to 12.

CHINESE PEPPER STEAK

One of the easiest versions, yet oh so good. Tastes equally good with or without soy sauce. Add red and yellow peppers for color.

Cooking oil	3 tbsp.	50 mL
Round steak cut in thin strips	2 lbs.	1 kg
All-purpose flour, to coat	¼ cup	50 mL
Salt	½ tsp.	2 mL
Pepper	⅛ tsp.	0.5 mL
Green peppers, seeded and thinly sliced	3	3
Medium onions, thinly sliced	2	2
Garlic clove, minced	1	1
Tomato sauce	7½ oz.	213 mL
Soy sauce	¼ cup	50 mL
Beef bouillon cube	1	1
Water	¼ cup	50 mL
Whole mushrooms and juice	10 oz.	284 mL

Heat oil in frying pan. Cut meat into short strips. Put in paper or plastic bag containing flour, salt and pepper. Shake to coat. Brown. Transfer to 2½ quart (3 L) casserole.

Put peppers, onions and garlic into pan. Sauté until soft.

Add tomato and soy sauce, beef cube, water, mushrooms and juice. Break up and dissolve cube. Pour over meat. Cover. Bake in 350°F (180°C) oven for 1 hour or more until very tender. Serves 8.

Note: This may be served on a bed of rice.

Pictured on back cover.

STEW IN A BASKET

An edible bowl! A sure way to impress.

BASKETS

Frozen bread loaves thawed, wholewheat or white	2	2
Aluminum foil deep pot pie plates 5 x 1³/₁₆ inches (12.5 x 3 cm)	8	8

Divide each bread loaf into 4 equal parts. Roll or pat and stretch each part into a 7 inch (18 cm) circle. Fit over outside of inverted greased foil dish. Let rise until soft and puffy feeling, about ½ hour. Bake in 375°F (190°C) oven for 15 to 20 minutes. Cool before removing from foil.

STEW

Cooking oil	2 tbsp.	30 mL
Stew meat, cut bite size	2 lbs.	1 kg
Water	1 cup	250 mL
Beef bouillon cube	1	1
Water	3 cups	750 mL
Seasoned salt	2 tsp.	10 mL
Pepper	¼ tsp.	1 mL
Thinly sliced carrots	2 cups	500 mL
Large onion, chunked	1	1
Sliced celery	1 cup	250 mL
Large potatoes	2	2
Canned cut green beans, drained	½ cup	125 mL
Canned sliced mushrooms, drained	½ cup	125 mL
Cornstarch	1 tbsp.	15 mL
Water	1 tbsp.	15 mL

Put cooking oil and ½ the meat into frying pan. Brown well. Transfer to large pot. Brown second ½ meat adding more oil if needed. Brown well since much flavor is added by doing so. Add to pot.

Pour first amount of water into frying pan. Scrape to dislodge any brown color and bits. Add beef cube. Stir to dissolve. Pour over meat.

(continued on next page)

Add second amount of water, salt and pepper to meat. Bring to a boil. Cover and simmer slowly for about 1½ hours until tender. Add more water if needed.

Add carrot, onion, celery and potato. Continue to simmer until vegetables are tender, about 30 minutes.

Add green beans and mushrooms.

Mix cornstarch and remaining water. Stir into simmering mixture to thicken. Repeat this amount if you prefer thicker gravy. Spoon into 8 baskets.

Note: To thicken with flour instead of cornstarch, use 2 tbsp. (30 mL) all-purpose flour mixed well with 3 tbsp. (50 mL) water.

Pictured on page 179.

TATER TOT CASSEROLE

So easy to prepare. So easy to eat. Meat is on the bottom with potatoes and sauce on top.

Lean ground beef	1½ lbs.	680 g
Condensed cream of celery soup	10 oz.	284 mL
Salt	1 tsp.	5 mL
Pepper	¼ tsp.	1 mL
Frozen potato tots, gems or puffs	½ lb.	250 g
Water	⅓ cup	75 mL

Combine beef and 5 oz. (141 mL) of the can of celery soup in bowl. Set aside remaining celery soup. Add salt and pepper to beef mixture. Mix well. Pack into 8 x 8 inch (20 x 20 cm) ungreased pan.

Arrange potato over meat, covering well.

Whisk remaining ½ can soup with water. Pour over potato. Bake uncovered in 350°F (180°C) oven for about 1 hour 15 minutes. Serves 4 to 6.

Pictured on page 71.

CHOW CHOW

A family favorite, this green tomato pickle goes especially well with any meat and gravy dish. Makes a good gift.

Onions, sliced	5 lbs.	3.2 kg
Green tomatoes, very firm, sliced	16 lbs.	7.2 kg
Salt	1 cup	250 mL
Granulated sugar	5 lbs.	2.2 kg
Pickling spice in bag	3 oz.	85 g
Turmeric	2 tbsp.	30 mL
Vinegar	1½ - 2 qts.	1.5 - 2 L

Peel onions. Slice in ¼ inch (.5 cm) slices. Cut up slices. Remove stem end from tomatoes. Slice in ¼ inch (.5 cm) slices. Cut up slices. Slicing tomatoes after onions will remove onion smell from hands. Layer tomatoes, onions and salt in large, heavy preserving kettle. Cover. Let stand overnight.

Next day drain well. Add sugar. Secure pickling spice in bag made of any clean fabric — unbleached cotton is good. Push bag down among tomatoes. Add turmeric. Pour on vinegar until it reaches about 1 inch (2.5 cm) below surface of tomatoes. Too much vinegar will make too much juice. Bring to a boil, stirring frequently. Simmer about 2 hours. Remove spice bag and discard. Adjust sugar now. Go by taste. Add more if not sweet enough. Add more turmeric if needed to make a pleasing color. Pour into clean, sterilized jars. Seal. Yield: 9 to 10 quarts (9 to 10 L) or the equivalent in small jars.

Note: Do not use enamel container to make Chow Chow as it will scorch on the bottom.

Pictured on page 71.

Paré Pointer

Batman and Robin were in front of a herd of stampeding cattle. There go the cattle. There lies Flatman and Ribbon.

CHEESEBURGER BAKE

A tasty dish for lunch or for an evening snack.

White bread slices, toasted, both sides buttered	8	8
Ground beef	1 lb.	450 g
Chopped onion	¼ cup	50 mL
Chopped celery	2 tbsp.	30 mL
Prepared mustard	1 tbsp.	15 mL
Salt	½ tsp.	2 mL
Shredded medium Cheddar cheese	1 cup	250 mL
Egg, fork beaten	1	1
Milk	¾ cup	175 mL
Salt	½ tsp.	2 mL
Pepper	⅛ tsp.	0.5 mL
Dry mustard	⅛ tsp.	0.5 mL
Paprika		

Arrange 4 toast slices in bottom of greased 9 x 9 inch (22 x 22 cm) pan. Set aside.

Put beef, onion, celery, mustard and salt into frying pan. Scramble fry until brown and onion is tender. Spread ½ of this mixture over toast in pan.

Sprinkle ½ of cheese over top. Arrange remaining toast slices over cheese. Spread with remaining meat mixture followed by second ½ of cheese.

Mix egg, milk, salt, pepper and mustard together. Pour over top.

Sprinkle with paprika. Bake uncovered in 350°F (180°C) oven for about 30 to 35 minutes. Serves 4 to 6.

Paré Pointer

You don't need presence of mind in a car accident nearly as much as absence of body.

BEEF AND CORN BAKE

Quick to assemble and really flavorful. A great zesty "take to the lake" dish.

Ground beef	2 lbs.	1 kg
Medium onion, chopped	1	1
Cooking oil	¼ cup	50 mL
Kernel corn	12 oz.	341 mL
Condensed tomato soup	2 x 10 oz.	2 x 284 mL
Salt	1 tsp.	5 mL
Pepper	½ tsp.	2 mL
Ketchup	1 tbsp.	15 mL
Cooked noodles	2 cups	500 mL
Grated Cheddar cheese	1 cup	250 mL

Put ground beef, onion and oil into frying pan. Stir to break up meat as it browns. Drain off fat. Discard. Put meat mixture into large bowl.

Put corn, soup, salt, pepper and ketchup into same bowl. Stir to mix together with meat.

Prepare noodles according to package directions. Drain. Measure. Combine with all ingredients in bowl. Pour into 3 quart (3.5 L) casserole.

Sprinkle grated cheese over top. Cover. Bake in 350°F (180°C) oven for 45 minutes. Remove cover and continue to bake until cheese is melted and bubbly. Serves 6 to 8.

Paré Pointer

If you are big you can be a cad. If you are small you can be a caddy.

68

An extra special treat when cost is no object.

Canned lobster	5 oz.	142 g
Canned shrimp	4 oz.	113 g
Canned crab	5 oz.	142 g
Canned chicken	6½ oz.	184 g
Scallops, fresh or frozen	½ lb.	250 g
Butter or margarine	½ cup	125 mL
All-purpose flour	½ cup	125 mL
Dry mustard	¼ tsp.	1 mL
Salt	½ tsp.	2 mL
Milk	2 cups	450 mL
Sour cream	1 cup	250 mL
Sherry or white wine (or apple juice)	½ cup	125 mL
Butter or margarine for topping	2 tbsp.	30 mL
Bread crumbs	1 cup	250 mL
Grated Cheddar cheese	½ cup	125 mL

Put lobster, shrimp, crab and chicken into large bowl. Break into bite size pieces, removing membrane.

Cover scallops with water in medium saucepan. Boil 5 minutes. Drain. Cut in half and add to bowl. Set aside.

In same saucepan, melt butter. Stir in flour, mustard and salt. Add milk. Cook, stirring, until mixture boils.

Add sour cream and sherry or wine. Pour over contents in bowl. Stir lightly to combine. Pour into 2½ quart (3L) casserole.

Melt butter in saucepan. Remove from heat. Stir in crumbs to coat. Add cheese. Stir lightly. Spread over top of casserole. Bake at 350° F (180° C) oven for 20 to 30 minutes until hot and bubbly. Serves 12.

Pare Pointer

Can it cost much to feed a horse? It eats best without a bit in its mouth.

BBQ PORK CHOPS

This is such a good way to serve pork chops. It will wait in the refrigerator until you are ready to bake it.

Pork chops	12	12
Medium onions, cut in slices and separated into rings	3	3
SAUCE		
Tomato juice	2 cups	450 mL
Vinegar	2 tbsp.	30 mL
Dry mustard	1 tsp.	5 mL
Worcestershire sauce	1 tbsp.	15 mL
Finely chopped onion	½ cup	125 mL
Chili powder	½ tsp.	2 mL
Salt	½ tsp.	2 mL
Dash of pepper		

Brown chops on both sides. Arrange in roaster or large casserole, covering each chop with sliced onion rings.

Sauce: Combine all sauce ingredients together in medium size saucepan. Bring to boil. Simmer slowly for 10 minutes. Pour over chops in roaster. Cover. Bake in 350° F (180° C) oven for 30 minutes. Remove cover and bake for 15 minutes more. Serves 6 people 2 chops each.

1. Chow Chow page 66
2. Beef Noodle Bake page 60
3. Tuna Pie page 60
4. Tater Tot Casserole page 65

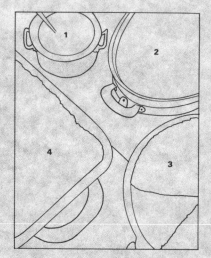

CANDIED CARROTS

The glaze makes these shiny and irresistible.

Carrots cut in irregular shaped pieces	2 lbs.	1 kg
Salted water		
Butter or margarine	1 tbsp.	15 mL
All-purpose flour	2 tsp.	10 mL
Brown sugar	2 tbsp.	30 mL
Prepared orange juice	½ cup	125 mL

Cook carrots in small amount of salted water until tender. Drain.

Meanwhile, melt butter in saucepan. Stir in flour and brown sugar. Add orange juice, stirring until mixture boils and thickens slightly. Pour over carrots. Stir to coat. Serves 8.

POTATOES EXTRAORDINAIRE

A wonderful make ahead that tastes fresh with all the trimmings. Can be made in the morning to be heated later in the day or can be prepared a day or more in advance. May be halved for fewer appetites. Can be frozen.

Potatoes	5 lbs.	2.27 kg
Cream cheese, softened	8 oz.	250 g
Sour cream	1 cup	250 mL
Butter or margarine, softened	¼ cup	50 mL
Onion salt	1 tbsp.	15 mL
Salt	1 tsp.	5 mL
Pepper	¼ tsp.	1 mL
Butter and paprika for garnish		

Cook potatoes as usual in salted water until tender. Drain. Mash well.

Add cream cheese in pieces. Add next 5 ingredients. Beat until smooth and fluffy. Scrape into 2 quart (2 L) casserole.

Place dabs of butter here and there over top of potatoes. Sprinkle with paprika. Cover and heat in 350°F (180°C) oven until heated through. Makes about 12 servings.

SALMON NEWBURG

Make this delicious lunch right from the shelf.

Grated onion	1 tbsp.	15 mL
Butter or margarine	2 tbsp.	30 mL
All-purpose flour	3 tbsp.	50 mL
Salt	½ tsp.	2 mL
Pepper	⅛ tsp.	0.5 mL
Paprika	⅛ tsp.	0.5 mL
Milk	1¼ cups	300 mL
Hot pepper sauce	⅛ tsp.	0.5 mL
Salmon, drained, skin and round bones removed	15 oz.	439 mL
Parsley flakes	1 tbsp.	15 mL
Egg yolks	2	2
Cream	¼ cup	50 mL
Sherry (optional)	1½ tsp.	7 mL

In medium size saucepan sauté onion in butter for about 5 minutes.

Add flour, salt, pepper and paprika. Mix together. Stir in milk and hot pepper sauce stirring until it boils and thickens.

Flake the salmon then add along with parsley. Simmer slowly for 2 to 3 minutes.

Put egg yolks, cream and sherry into small container. Beat well with fork to blend. Stir into salmon mixture. Simmer slowly for about 2 minutes more. Serve over toast, rice or puffed pastry shells. Serves 4.

MUSHROOM SAUCE

Butter or margarine	6 tbsp.	100 mL
Chopped onion	½ cup	125 mL
Fresh mushrooms, sliced	8 - 10	8 - 10
All-purpose flour	¼ cup	50 mL
Salt	½ tsp.	2 mL
Pepper	⅛ tsp.	0.5 mL
Dry dill weed	¼ tsp.	1 mL
Milk	2 cups	500 mL

(continued on next page)

Melt butter in saucepan. Add onion and mushrooms. Sauté until onions are soft.

Mix in flour, salt, pepper and dill weed. Stir in milk slowly, small quantities at a time, until it boils and thickens. Use up to 2 cups (500 mL) or less for a thicker sauce. Spoon over shells.

Pictured on page 215.

TUNA BAKE

The cheese flavor comes through in this wholesome meal-in-one dish.

Macaroni, raw	¾ cup	175 mL
Condensed cream of celery soup	10 oz.	284 mL
Milk	⅓ cup	75 mL
Peas, frozen or fresh	1½ cups	350 mL
Cheese slices, broken up	4	4
Salt	½ tsp.	2 mL
Dash of pepper		
Tuna	7 oz.	198 g
Cheese slices for top	2	2

Cook macaroni as directed on package. Rinse with cold water. Drain. Pour into greased 1½ quart (1.5 L) casserole. Set aside.

In medium size saucepan combine soup, milk, peas and cheese slices. Heat and stir until hot and cheese is melted. Add salt and pepper to taste. Pour over macaroni.

Drain tuna. Break up into pieces and put on top of sauce. Stir lightly to combine all together. Cover. Bake in 350°F (180°C) oven for 20 minutes.

Remove cover. Cut cheese slices diagonally to make 4 triangles. Arrange over casserole. Bake uncovered 5 minutes or until cheese is melted. Serves 4.

Paré Pointer

What can you expect from bad chickens except devilled eggs?

VEGETABLE DISH

A whole head of cauliflower topped with cheese sauce and surrounded with brussels sprouts. Make more sauce if desired.

Medium head of cauliflower	1	1
Salted water		
Brussels sprouts	1½ lbs.	700 g
Salted water		
CHEESE SAUCE		
Butter or margarine	¼ cup	60 mL
All-purpose flour	¼ cup	60 mL
Salt	½ tsp.	2 mL
Pepper	⅛ tsp.	0.5 mL
Milk	2 cups	500 mL
Process cheese spread	½ cup	125 mL

Remove leaves from cauliflower. Place whole head into salted water in saucepan. Cook until tender crisp. Drain and set in center of serving dish.

Trim sprouts. Cook in salted water until barely tender. Drain. Arrange around cauliflower.

Cheese Sauce: While vegetables are cooking, melt butter in saucepan. Mix in flour, salt and pepper.

Stir in milk until it boils and thickens. Add cheese. Stir to melt. More or less cheese may be added to taste. Taste for salt and pepper. Spoon over cauliflower. May be poured over sprouts as well. Serves 8.

Pictured on back cover.

CHICKEN HURRY

One of the quickest to assemble with no prebrowning.

Chicken parts	3 lbs.	1.4 kg
Ketchup	½ cup	125 mL
Water	¼ cup	50 mL
Brown sugar, packed	¼ cup	50 mL
Envelope dry onion soup mix	1½ oz.	42.5 g

(continued on next page)

Arrange chicken parts in small roaster or casserole.

In small bowl, combine ketchup, water, sugar and soup mix. Mix together well. Spoon over chicken making sure some is on every piece. Bake covered in 350°F (180°C) oven for at least 1 hour until very tender. Serves 4 to 6.

HASH BROWN PIZZA

Just a fantastic aroma followed by a fantastic flavor. A must to try. Everyone will rave about it.

Frozen hash browns, thawed	36 oz.	1 kg
Cheddar cheese soup	10 oz.	284 mL
Egg	1	1
Salt	1 tsp.	5 mL
Pepper	½ tsp.	2 mL
Ground beef	1 lb.	450 g
Finely chopped onion	2 tbsp.	30 mL
All-purpose flour	2 tbsp.	30 mL
Condensed cream of tomato soup	10 oz.	284 mL
Granulated sugar	2 tsp.	10 mL
Salt	½ tsp.	2 mL
Pepper	⅛ tsp.	0.5 mL
Garlic powder	¼ tsp.	1 mL
Grated Cheddar cheese	2 cups	500 mL

In large bowl mix first 5 ingredients together. Spread on greased 12 inch (30 cm) pizza pan. Pack well, forming a slight edge around outside. Bake in 450°F (230°C) oven for 20 to 25 minutes.

Scramble fry ground beef and onion in frying pan until browned.

Sprinkle with flour, stir. Add tomato soup, sugar, salt, pepper and garlic powder. Stir until it boils and thickens.

Sprinkle ⅔ of the grated cheese over potato base. Spoon meat mixture over cheese. Top with remaining cheese. Return to 450°F (230°C) oven for 5 minutes until cheese is melted and bubbly. Cut into 6 good size wedges to serve.

Pictured on page 89.

TUNA CASSEROLE

Just right for a planned or a spur-of-the-moment meal. Can be doubled easily.

Condensed cream of mushroom soup	10 oz.	284 mL
Water	¼ cup	50 mL
Chow mein noodles	1 cup	250 mL
Tuna	7 oz.	198 g
Sliced celery	1 cup	250 mL
Chopped onion	1 cup	250 mL
Chow mein noodles		

In 1½ quart (1.5 L) casserole, put soup, water and first amount of noodles. Toss together.

Drain tuna and add along with sliced celery and onion. Mix together lightly.

Cover top with extra noodles. Bake uncovered in 375° F (190° C) oven for 45 minutes or microwave on high power for 9 minutes. Serves 4.

To make this super special, add 1 cup (225 mL) salted, toasted cashew nuts to casserole ingredients.

HAMBURGER PATTY CASSEROLE

This can be made ahead. Reheats beautifully with a tasty gravy.

Ground beef	2½ lbs.	1.1 kg
Envelope dry onion soup mix	1½ oz.	42.5 g
Bread crumbs	1 cup	250 mL
Water	1 cup	250 mL
Salt	½ tsp.	2 mL
Condensed tomato soup	2 x 10 oz.	2 x 284 mL
Cans of water	2 x 10 oz.	2 x 284 mL
Mushroom pieces and juice	10 oz.	284 mL

(continued on next page)

Put first 5 ingredients into large bowl. Using your hand, mix together well. Shape into patties. Brown both sides in frying pan. Remove to baking dish.

Stir soup and water together in medium bowl. Stir in mushrooms and juice. Pour over meat. Bake covered in 350°F (180°C) oven for 1 hour. Serves 8.

LAZY PEROGY CASSEROLE

This streamlined version gets flavor without frenzy.

Lasagne noodles	15	15
Cottage cheese	2 cups	500 mL
Egg	1	1
Onion salt	¼ tsp.	1 mL
Shredded Cheddar cheese	1 cup	250 mL
Mashed potato	2 cups	500 mL
Salt	¼ tsp.	1 mL
Onion salt	¼ tsp.	1 mL
Pepper	⅛ tsp.	0.5 mL
Butter or margarine	1 cup	250 mL
Chopped onions	1 cup	250 mL

Cook noodles as directed on package. Drain. Line bottom of 9 x 13 inch (22 x 33 cm) pan.

In medium size bowl, mix cottage cheese, egg and onion salt together. Spoon over noodles and spread. Cover with layer of noodles.

In same bowl, mix Cheddar cheese with potato, salt, onion salt and pepper. Spread over noodles. Cover with layer of noodles.

Melt butter in frying pan. Sauté onions slowly until clear and soft. Pour over noodles. Cover. Bake 30 minutes in 350°F (180°C) oven. Let stand 10 minutes before cutting. Serve with sour cream. Makes 8 large servings.

PEAS AND PODS

Make those peas extra special.

Frozen peas	10 oz.	284 g
Frozen Chinese pea pods	6 oz.	170 g
Granulated sugar	½ tsp.	2 mL
Salted water		
Butter or margarine	2 tbsp.	30 mL

Cook all peas and sugar together in salted water until done. Drain.

Add butter. Toss lightly to melt and coat peas. Serves 4 to 6.

NO-FUSS STROGANOFF

A really delicious gourmet casserole made from hamburger.

Butter or margarine	2 tbsp.	30 mL
Finely chopped onion	1 cup	250 mL
Ground beef	1 lb.	500 g
All-purpose flour	2 tbsp.	30 mL
Salt	1 tsp.	5 mL
Pepper	¼ tsp.	1 mL
Sliced mushrooms, drained	10 oz.	284 mL
Condensed cream of chicken soup	10 oz.	284 mL
Sour cream	½ cup	125 mL
Grated Cheddar cheese	¼ cup	65 mL

Melt butter in frying pan. Add onions and sauté slowly until limp. Add beef stirring to break up lumps. Brown. Drain off fat. Discard.

Sprinkle flour, salt and pepper over meat mixture. Stir. Add mushrooms. Cook uncovered for 10 minutes.

Add soup. Stir. Cook uncovered for 10 minutes.

Stir in sour cream and cheese. Heat through. Can be served immediately or poured into a casserole, covered and held in warm oven. Serves 4.

Serve this egg and cheese pizza with or without toppings. A store-bought pizza crust speeds it up even more.

Tea biscuit mix	2¼ cups	550 mL
Milk	½ cup	125 mL
Butter or margarine	2 tbsp.	30 mL
Eggs	10	10
Water or milk	¼ cup	50 mL
Salt	1 tsp.	5 mL
Pepper	¼ tsp.	1 mL
Pizza or spaghetti sauce	½ cup	125 mL
Grated mozzarella cheese	2 cups	500 mL
Bacon pieces (partly cooked), ham, hot or plain sausage (cooked)		
Fresh mushrooms, sliced		
Sliced tomato		

Mix tea biscuit mix and milk together to make a soft dough. Pat onto greased 12 inch (30 cm) pizza pan. Bake in 375°F (190°C) oven for 15 minutes to partially cook.

Melt butter in frying pan. Add eggs, water, salt and pepper. Beat lightly with spoon to mix. Stir until cooked. Remove from heat.

Spread pizza sauce over crust in pan. Cover with scrambled eggs.

Sprinkle with grated cheese. Add any other toppings you prefer. Return to oven. Continue to bake for about 15 minutes or until topping is sizzling hot. Cuts into 8 pieces.

Paré Pointer

To safeguard your mental health never play a game of marbles. If you lose them you're in trouble.

CHEESE AND PASTA IN A POT

A good dish for a party. Have it ready in the refrigerator then pop it in the oven and join the party. When you have made it once the length of the recipe seems cut in half the second time.

Large shell macaroni	8 oz.	225 g
Ground beef	2 lbs.	1 kg
Medium onions, chopped	2	2
Garlic powder	¼ tsp.	1 mL
Canned stewed tomatoes	14 oz.	398 mL
Canned spaghetti sauce	14 oz.	398 mL
Mushroom pieces and juice	10 oz.	284 mL
Sour cream	2 cups	500 mL
Medium Cheddar cheese	½ lb.	250 g
Mozzarella cheese	½ lb.	250 g

Cook macaroni according to package directions. Rinse with cold water. Drain. Set aside.

Brown beef in frying pan. Drain and put in large saucepan such as a Dutch oven. Add onions, garlic, tomatoes, spaghetti sauce, mushrooms and juice. Bring to boil and allow to simmer 20 minutes until onions are tender. Stir occasionally while boiling. Remove from heat. Use 4 quart (5 L) casserole or roaster.

Construction:
1. Pour one half macaroni in bottom of casserole
2. Pour over one half meat sauce
3. Spread with one half sour cream
4. Slice Cheddar cheese thinly and layer half on top
5. Cover with second half of macaroni
6. Spoon over second half of meat sauce
7. Spread with second half of sour cream
8. Cover with remaining thin slices of Cheddar cheese
9. Top with thin slices of mozzarella cheese

Cover. Bake in 350° F (180° C) oven for 45 minutes. Remove cover. Continue baking until cheese is melted. Allow more baking time if chilled and held. Serves 12.

Serve elegant meatballs with universal appeal.

Ground beef	2 lbs.	1 kg
Bread crumbs	1 cup	250 mL
Water	1 cup	250 mL
Salt	2 tsp.	10 mL
Pepper	½ tsp.	2 mL
Water	2 cups	450 mL
Small onion, finely chopped	1	1
Instant beef in a mug soup powder	¼ cup	50 mL
Salt	1 tsp.	5 mL
Pepper	¼ tsp.	1 mL
Cornstarch	4 tbsp.	50 mL
Water	¼ cup	50 mL
Sliced mushrooms	10 oz.	284 mL
Condensed cream of mushroom soup	10 oz.	284 mL
Dry parsley flakes	2 tsp.	10 mL
Paprika	¼ tsp.	2 mL
Sour cream	2 cups	500 mL

In large bowl mix beef, crumbs, water, salt and pepper. Shape into about 40 meatballs. Put on cookie sheet with sides. Bake in 425°F (220°C) oven for 15 minutes. Pile into casserole.

In medium saucepan put water, onion, soup powder, salt and pepper. Bring to boil.

In small bowl, stir cornstarch into water. Pour into boiling liquid stirring until thickened.

Stir in mushrooms, soup, parsley, paprika and sour cream. If too thick stir in a bit of water.

Pour over meatballs. Cover. Bake in 350°F (180°C) oven for 25 to 30 minutes until heated through. Serves 6.

Paré Pointer

No more eggs for you. We hens are tired of working for chicken feed.

SALMON BALL CASSEROLE

This is one of the most appetizing ways of serving salmon. Make the balls smaller if using as a second meat. Pink salmon works fine. Use red if you want more color.

Canned salmon	2 x 7¾ oz.	2 x 220 g
Long-grain rice, raw	½ cup	125 mL
Grated carrot	½ cup	125 mL
Chopped onion	¼ cup	50 mL
Egg	1	1
Salt	½ tsp.	2 mL
Pepper	⅛ tsp.	0.5 mL
Condensed cream of mushroom soup	10 oz.	284 mL
Water	½ cup	125 mL

Put salmon and juice into medium size bowl. Remove skin and round bones.

Add rice, carrot, onion, egg, salt and pepper. Mix together well. Shape into balls and put in casserole leaving room for expansion. Sixteen balls are just right for 9 x 9 inch (23 x 23 cm) dish.

Mix soup and water together. Pour over top. Bake covered in oven at 350°F (180°C) for about 1 hour. Serves 5 to 6.

CARMAN'S CAPER

Just a really good anytime casserole. Quick and easy to assemble.

Ground beef	1½ lbs.	750 g
Chopped onion	½ cup	125 mL
Salt	1½ tsp.	7 mL
Pepper	¼ tsp.	1 mL
Spaghetti	½ lb.	250 g
Canned tomatoes	19 oz.	540 mL
Condensed cream of mushroom soup	10 oz.	284 mL
Grated Cheddar cheese	1 cup	250 mL

(continued on next page)

Brown beef and onion in frying pan. Sprinkle with salt and pepper. Stir. Transfer to bottom of 2 quart (2 L) casserole.

Break up spaghetti for easier serving. Cook according to package directions. Drain. Layer over meat.

Break up large tomato chunks. Pour over top. Spoon soup over tomatoes. Cover with cheese. Bake uncovered in 350°F (180°C) oven for 30 minutes until hot and cheese is melted. Cover halfway through cooking if cheese starts getting dry. Serves 6.

SWEET POTATO CASSEROLE

May be prepared ahead. Just reheat and serve. This has a beautiful glaze.

Sweet potatoes, peeled, cooked and cut into irregular shaped pieces	2½ lbs.	1.1 kg
Brown sugar, packed	½ cup	125 mL
Butter or margarine	2 tbsp.	30 mL
Cornstarch	1½ tbsp.	25 mL
Salt	½ tsp.	2 mL
Pepper	⅛ tsp.	0.5 mL
Prepared orange juice	1 cup	250 mL

Cut potatoes into bite size pieces and place in 2 quart (2 L) casserole.

Mix remaining ingredients in saucepan. Heat and stir until it boils and thickens. Pour over potatoes. Cover and bake in 350°F (180°C) oven for 20 minutes. Remove cover for last few minutes if desired. Serves 8.

Note: This can be made using 2 cans, 19 oz. (540 mL) each, drained sweet potatoes, cut into chunks.

Pare Pointer

A worn out rifle is otherwise known as a shot gun.

SWEET AND SOUR MEATBALLS

This fits in well as a second meat. Its tangy taste goes with anything.

Ground beef	1¼ lbs.	550 g
Bread crumbs	½ cup	125 mL
Water or milk	½ cup	125 mL
Salt	1 tsp.	5 mL
Pepper	¼ tsp.	1 mL
Brown sugar, packed	2 cups	500 mL
All-purpose flour	2 tbsp.	30 mL
Vinegar	½ cup	125 mL
Water	¼ cup	65 mL
Soy sauce	2 tbsp.	30 mL
Ketchup	1 tbsp.	15 mL

In medium size bowl, mix beef, crumbs, water, salt and pepper. Shape into approximately 24 balls. Brown in frying pan or hot oven. Transfer to casserole.

In medium size saucepan put brown sugar and flour. Stir well to blend thoroughly.

Add vinegar, water, soy sauce and ketchup. Stir over medium-high heat until boiling. Pour over meatballs. Cover. Heat in 350°F (180°C) oven for 20 minutes until hot and bubbly. Serves 4.

Paré Pointer

Contrary to what you may have heard, if you have a bad temper it is best to lose it.

CHINESE HEKKA

This is an extra good Chinese casserole. A very full flavor, it is traditionally served with lots of rice.

Ground beef	1¼ lbs.	550 g
Chopped onion	1¼ cups	300 mL
Cooking oil	2 tbsp.	30 mL
Shredded cabbage	2 cups	500 mL
Shredded carrots	2 cups	500 mL
Sliced celery	2 cups	500 mL
Soy sauce	½ cup	125 mL
Water	½ cup	125 mL

Put beef, onion and oil into frying pan. Brown, stirring to break up meat. Drain off fat and discard. Remove from heat.

Shred cabbage using large size grater. Shred carrots using small size grater. Slice celery in thin angle slices. Add cabbage, carrots, celery, soy sauce and water to meat and onions. Scrape into 1½ quart (1.5 L) casserole. Cover. Bake in 350° F (180° C) oven for 45 minutes. Serves 6.

SOUPER SUPPER

Brightens up your table with each colorful ingredient showing through.

Condensed cream of mushroom soup	10 oz.	284 mL
Soup can of water	10 oz.	284 mL
Soup can of minute rice	10 oz.	284 mL
Chopped cooked broccoli	1½ cups	350 mL
Cheese slices, cut up	4	4
Ham, cooked and cut up	1½ cups	350 mL

Put soup, water and rice into casserole. Mix together.

Add broccoli, cheese pieces and ham. Stir to distribute evenly. Cover. Bake in 350° F (180° C) oven for 30 minutes. Serves 6.

CURRIED RICE

Makes a great extra. Nice aroma. Looks pretty. Really good.

Minute rice, uncooked	2 cups	450 mL
Butter or margarine	1 tbsp.	15 mL
All-purpose flour	1 tbsp.	15 mL
Milk	1½ cups	350 mL
Salad dressing	½ cup	125 mL
Curry powder	½ tsp.	2 mL
Chopped pimiento	2 tbsp.	30 mL
Instant onion flakes	1 tbsp.	15 mL
Canned shrimp, small size, drained	4 oz.	113 g

Prepare rice as directed on package. Put into shallow baking dish. Keep warm.

In medium saucepan, melt butter. Stir in flour. Add milk. Bring to boil, stirring. Will be fairly thin.

Add salad dressing, curry, pimiento and onion.

Drain shrimp. Stir shrimp into sauce. Mix and pour evenly over rice. Stir fork here and there to allow some sauce to penetrate. Ready to serve. Or cover and put into warm oven to hold. Serves 12 as an extra. Add extra ¼ cup (50 mL) milk if held in oven.

1. Layered Turkey Salad page 156
2. Hash Brown Pizza page 77
3. Lasagne page 61

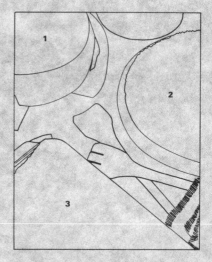

BEV'S CHICKEN CASSEROLE

A real winner. So simple to assemble, it is hard to believe it ends up as a gourmet dish. Although traditionally served with rice the sauce is delicious over mashed potatoes.

Chicken pieces, skin removed	3 lbs.	1.4 kg
Garlic powder	½ - ¾ tsp.	3 - 4 mL
Salt	1 tsp.	5 mL
Pepper	¼ tsp.	1 mL
Condensed tomato soup	10 oz.	284 mL
Condensed cream of mushroom soup	10 oz.	284 mL
Bunch green onions and tops, finely cut	1	1
Small onion, chopped	1	1
Fresh tomato, chopped	1	1

Arrange chicken pieces in bottom of large casserole or small roaster. Sprinkle with garlic, salt and pepper.

Combine both soups with onions and tomato. Spoon over chicken. Cover. Bake in 350°F (180°C) oven for 2 hours or until tender. Serves 4.

She never did a crossword puzzle because she feared hard feelings. One word leads to another.

SHORT RIBS

Who would have thought you could make company fare from plain short ribs?

Short ribs	3 - 4 lbs.	1.4 - 1.8 kg
SAUCE		
Tomato sauce	7½ oz.	213 mL
Salt	1½ tsp.	7 mL
Pepper	½ tsp.	2 mL
Dried onion flakes	1 tbsp.	15 mL
Molasses	2 tbsp.	30 mL
Vinegar	2 tbsp.	30 mL

Place ribs into large casserole or medium roaster.

Sauce: Combine all sauce ingredients in small bowl. Mix together well. Pour over ribs. Cover. Bake in 300°F (160°C) oven for 4 to 5 hours until tender. Remove meat to serving bowl. Tip pan slightly and skim off fat before dishing sauce over top. Serves 4.

BARBECUED RIBS

Enjoy a kitchen barbecue.

Meaty spareribs	4 lbs.	1.8 kg
Cooking oil	3 tbsp.	45 mL
Large onion, chopped	1	1
Ketchup	1 cup	225 mL
Water	1 cup	225 mL
Vinegar	½ cup	125 mL
Brown sugar, packed	½ cup	125 mL
Worcestershire sauce	1 tsp.	5 mL
Salt	1 tsp.	5 mL

Cut ribs into serving pieces. Brown in oil in frying pan or under broiler. Put in large roaster.

In medium size bowl combine onion, ketchup, water, vinegar, sugar, Worcestershire and salt. Stir. Pour evenly over ribs. Cover. Bake in 350°F (180°C) oven for 2 hours. Remove cover. Continue to cook for 15 minutes. Serves 6.

WINDMILLS

Decorative as well as tasty. Try jam with some and top others with half a cherry.

Butter or margarine, softened	½ cup	125 mL
Granulated sugar	¾ cup	175 mL
Eggs	2	2
Vanilla	1 tsp.	5 mL
All-purpose flour	2 cups	500 mL
Baking powder	1 tsp.	5 mL
Salt	¼ tsp.	1 mL
Raspberry or strawberry jam	9 tbsp.	135 mL
Small pecan halves	54	54

Cream butter and sugar together. Beat in eggs and vanilla.

Stir flour, baking powder and salt together and add. Mix well. Roll on lightly floured surface. Cut into 3 inch (8 cm) squares. Cut 1½ inch (4 cm) slits in from each corner. Fold each corner in same direction to center.

Place ¼ tsp. (1 mL) jam in center. Top with pecan or a few chopped nuts or leave with jam only. Bake on ungreased sheet in 400°F (200°C) oven for about 6 minutes. Makes 4½ dozen.

Pictured on page 107.

PEANUT CEREAL STACKS

Quick to prepare this firm, chewy cookie.

Smooth peanut butter	½ cup	125 mL
Granulated sugar	½ cup	125 mL
Evaporated milk	¼ cup	60 mL
Cornflakes	2½ cups	625 mL

Put peanut butter, sugar and milk into bowl. Blend together until smooth. Add cornflakes. Mix well to coat evenly. Drop by teaspoon-fuls onto ungreased cookie sheet. Bake in 375°F (190°C) oven until browned, about 6 minutes. Makes about 2½ dozen.

Pictured on page 107.

CREAMY SNOWBALLS

If you have a sweet tooth these are for you. Creamy.

Cream cheese, softened	4 oz.	125 g
Icing (confectioner's) sugar	2 cups	500 mL
Milk	2 tbsp.	30 mL
Semisweet chocolate chips, melted	²/₃ cup	150 mL
Vanilla	½ tsp.	2 mL
Miniature colored marshmallows	3 cups	750 mL
Coconut		

Combine first 5 ingredients together in bowl. Beat together until smooth.

Fold in marshmallows. Chill well. Shape into 1¼ inch (3 cm) balls.

Roll in coconut. These freeze well. Makes about 3½ dozen.

Pictured on page 107.

COTTAGE CHEESE FUDGE COOKIES

Rolling these in powdered sugar before baking gives an attractive crackled appearance. Soft and cake-like. A good way to use cottage cheese.

Butter or margarine, softened	²/₃ cup	150 mL
Granulated sugar	1²/₃ cups	400 mL
Cottage cheese	1 cup	250 mL
Eggs	2	2
Vanilla	2 tsp.	10 mL
All-purpose flour	2¼ cups	550 mL
Cocoa	¾ cup	175 mL
Baking powder	1 tsp.	5 mL
Baking soda	½ tsp.	2 mL
Chopped almonds or walnuts	½ cup	125 mL
Icing (confectioner's) sugar		

(continued on next page)

Beat butter and sugar together. Beat in cottage cheese. Add eggs 1 at a time beating after each addition. Add vanilla.

Add flour, cocoa, baking powder, baking soda and nuts. Mix well. Roll into 1 inch (2.5 cm) balls.

Roll balls in icing sugar. Place on greased baking sheet. Bake in 350° F (180° C) oven for about 12 minutes until they feel firm. Makes 6 dozen.

Pictured on page 107.

TURTLE COOKIES

Snappy and cute. A birthday party special.

Butter or margarine, softened	½ cup	125 mL
Brown sugar, packed	½ cup	125 mL
Egg	1	1
Egg yolk	1	1
Vanilla	¼ tsp.	1 mL
Maple flavoring	⅛ tsp.	0.5 mL
All-purpose flour	1½ cups	375 mL
Baking soda	¼ tsp.	1 mL
Salt	¼ tsp.	1 mL
Egg white, fork beaten	1	1
Pecan halves, split	1½ cups	375 mL
Semisweet chocolate chips		

Cream butter and sugar together. Beat in egg, yolk and flavorings.

Stir in flour, baking soda and salt. Shape into 1 inch (2.5 cm) balls.

Place 3 nut pieces on greased cookie sheet to form head and 2 front legs plus 2 pieces for back legs.

Dip bottom of ball into egg white. Place in center of shaped nuts. Flatten slightly. Bake in 350° F (180° C) oven for 10 to 12 minutes. Cool.

Place 6 to 8 semisweet chocolate chips on each hot cookie. Allow them to melt, then spread with knife. Chocolate icing may be used as an alternative. Makes 3½ dozen.

Pictured on page 107.

CHOCOLATE CREAM DROPS

A very mellow chocolate flavor. Tops.

Butter or margarine, softened	1 cup	250 mL
Cream cheese, softened	4 oz.	125 g
Granulated sugar	1½ cups	375 mL
Egg	1	1
Milk	2 tbsp.	30 mL
Vanilla	½ tsp.	2 mL
Unsweetened chocolate squares, melted	2 x 1 oz.	2 x 28 g
Cake flour	2½ cups	600 mL
Baking powder	1½ tsp.	7 mL
Salt	¼ tsp.	1 mL
Chopped walnuts	½ cup	125 mL

Cream butter, cheese and sugar together well. Beat in egg, milk, vanilla and chocolate.

Stir remaining ingredients together and add. Mix well. Drop by spoonfuls onto greased baking sheet. Bake in 350°F (180°C) oven for 10 to 12 minutes. To have a continuing supply of these, pack in layers in plastic container while still a bit warm, with plastic wrap in between layers. Cover with lid and freeze. When removed to serve, they are moist and luscious. Makes 5 dozen.

OATMEAL COOKIES

So caramely tasting. A great cookie jar type.

Eggs	2	2
Brown sugar, packed	1 cup	250 mL
Granulated sugar	½ cup	125 mL
Cooking oil	1 cup	250 mL
Vanilla	1 tsp.	5 mL
Baking soda	1 tsp.	5 mL
Hot water	1 tbsp.	15 mL
Rolled oats	2 cups	500 mL
All-purpose flour	1½ cups	375 mL
Salt	1 tsp.	5 mL

(continued on next page)

Beat eggs in mixing bowl until frothy. Beat in both sugars. Add cooking oil and vanilla.

Dissolve baking soda in hot water. Stir in.

Add oats, flour and salt. Stir well. Drop by spoonfuls onto greased baking sheet. Bake in 350°F (180°C) oven for about 8 minutes. Makes 3½ dozen.

RAISIN OATMEAL: Add 1 cup (250 mL) raisins. If you would like spice too, add 1 tsp. (5 mL) cinnamon, ¼ tsp. (1 mL) nutmeg and ¼ tsp. (1 mL) allspice. Nuts are optional, ½ cup (125 mL).

PEANUT BUTTER COOKIES

Makes a huge batch but can easily be halved. Certain children have been raised on these. A family favorite. One serving is as many as can be held between thumb and index finger.

Butter or margarine, softened	1 cup	250 mL
Brown sugar, packed	1 cup	250 mL
Granulated sugar	1 cup	250 mL
Eggs	2	2
Smooth peanut butter	1 cup	250 mL
All-purpose flour	3 cups	750 mL
Baking soda	2 tsp.	10 mL
Salt	¼ tsp.	1 mL

Cream butter and both sugars together. Beat in eggs, 1 at a time. Mix in peanut butter.

Stir in flour, baking soda and salt. Shape into small balls. Place on ungreased cookie sheets allowing room for expansion. Press with fork. Dip fork in flour as needed to prevent batter stickiness. Bake in 375°F (190°C) oven for 12 to 15 minutes. Makes 6 dozen.

Pictured on page 107.

PEANUT BUTTER CHIP COOKIES: Add 1 to 2 cups (250 to 500 mL) semisweet chocolate chips.

PEANUT BUTTER JELLY NESTS: Shape dough into 1 inch (2.5 cm) balls. Place on cookie sheet. Press with thumb to indent. Bake in 375°F (190°C) oven for 5 minutes. Press again. Bake for 7 to 10 minutes more. Fill with red raspberry or strawberry jelly while cookies are still warm or store and fill as needed.

QUICK DATE FILLED COOKIES

An easy way to make oatmeal cookies.

COOKIES

Rolled oats	3 cups	750 mL
Brown sugar, packed	1 cup	250 mL
All-purpose flour	1 cup	250 mL
Salt	½ tsp.	2 mL
Vanilla	1 tsp.	5 mL
Butter or margarine, melted	1 cup	250 mL
Boiling water	¼ cup	60 mL
Baking soda	1 tsp.	5 mL

FILLING

Chopped dates	½ lb.	250 g
Granulated sugar	⅓ cup	75 mL
Water	⅔ cup	150 mL

Cookies: Measure first 6 ingredients into mixing bowl. Mix together well.

Stir water and baking soda together. Add. Mix well. Shape into 2 inch (5 cm) rolls. Wrap and chill. Dough may also be frozen. When ready to bake slice thinly. Place on ungreased pan. Bake in 375°F (190°C) oven for 8 to 10 minutes Makes 4 dozen.

Filling: Combine dates, sugar and water in saucepan. Bring to boil, simmer, stirring often, until mushy. Add more water if too dry. If too runny simmer longer to evaporate moisture. Cool and spread between cookies.

Paré Pointer

If you cross a witch and a millionaire you would have a witch person.

CHOCOLATE ROLL

This is a colorful confection. It freezes well. After a few slices are cut, you can pop it back in the refrigerator or freezer. The icing sugar gives it a very smooth texture.

Semisweet chocolate chips	1 cup	250 mL
Butter or margarine	2 tbsp.	30 mL
Egg, beaten	1	1
Icing (confectioner's) sugar	1 cup	250 mL
Small colored marshmallows	2½ cups	625 mL
Maraschino cherries, quartered	½ cup	125 mL
Chopped walnuts	½ cup	125 mL
Coconut for coating		

Melt chips and butter in large heavy saucepan over low heat. Remove from heat.

Add beaten egg, icing sugar, marshmallows, well-drained and quartered cherries and walnuts. Stir to mix. Cool if very warm. Form mixture into a roll.

Sprinkle some coconut over counter top, in space big enough to move roll around to coat with coconut. After well coated, wrap in either waxed paper or plastic. Chill well before attempting to slice. Slice thinly with clean sharp knife.

PEANUT BUTTER CUPS

A real treat for any age. Takes extra time to dip in chocolate.

Smooth peanut butter	1½ cups	375 mL
Butter or margarine, softened	¼ cup	60 mL
Icing (confectioner's) sugar	2 cups	500 mL
Vanilla	1 tsp.	5 mL
Semisweet chocolate chips	2 cups	500 mL
Grated parowax (paraffin)	⅓ cup	75 mL

Mix first 4 ingredients together. Shape into 1 inch (2.5 cm) balls. May be shaped into logs as well using same amount of dough.

Melt chocolate chips and wax in small heavy saucepan over low heat. Dip balls, drain and place on waxed paper. Makes about 7½ dozen.

SPICY DADS

A spicy version of the commercial variety.

Butter or margarine, softened	1 cup	250 mL
Granulated sugar	1 cup	250 mL
Brown sugar, packed	½ cup	125 mL
Egg	1	1
Molasses	2 tbsp.	30 mL
Vanilla	1 tsp.	5 mL
All-purpose flour	1½ cups	375 mL
Rolled oats	1½ cups	375 mL
Coconut	1 cup	250 mL
Baking powder	1 tsp.	5 mL
Baking soda	1 tsp.	5 mL
Cinnamon	1 tsp.	5 mL
Nutmeg	1 tsp.	5 mL
Allspice	1 tsp.	5 mL

Cream butter and both sugars together. Beat in egg. Add molasses and vanilla.

Stir remaining ingredients together and add. Mix well. Drop by spoonfuls onto greased baking sheet. Press with floured fork. Bake in 300°F (150°C) oven until golden, about 12 minutes. Makes 6 dozen.

Pictured on page 107.

TING A LINGS

Makes a crunchy chocolaty no-bake cookie.

Semisweet chocolate chips	1 cup	250 mL
Butter or margarine	2 tbsp.	30 mL
Corn flakes	1 cup	250 mL
Medium or long coconut	½ cup	125 mL
Peanuts	½ cup	125 mL
Vanilla	1 tsp.	5 mL

Melt chocolate chips and butter over low heat. Stir until smooth. Remove from heat.

Stir in remaining ingredients. Drop by small spoonfuls onto waxed paper. Chill. Makes 2 dozen.

Pictured on page 107.

CHOCOLATE CHIPPERS

These chocolate chip cookies are tops. A drop cookie that doesn't flatten too much.

Butter or margarine, softened	1 cup	250 mL
Brown sugar, packed	1½ cups	375 mL
Eggs	2	2
Vanilla	1 tsp.	5 mL
All-purpose flour	2 cups	500 mL
Cornstarch	¼ cup	60 mL
Salt	¾ tsp.	4 mL
Baking soda	1 tsp.	5 mL
Semisweet chocolate chips	2 cups	500 mL
Chopped walnuts (optional)	1 cup	250 mL

Cream butter and sugar together. Beat in eggs 1 at a time. Add vanilla.

Stir flour, cornstarch, salt and baking soda together and add. Stir in chips and nuts. Drop by spoonfuls onto greased baking sheet. Bake in 350°F (180°C) oven for 10 to 15 minutes. Makes 5½ dozen.

Pictured on page 107.

LEMON JELLY COOKIES

The gelatin powder gives these crunchy good cookies a mild lemon flavor. Pretty yellow color.

Butter or margarine, softened	¾ cup	175 mL
Granulated sugar	1 cup	250 mL
Lemon flavored gelatin powder	3 oz.	85 g
Eggs	2	2
All-purpose flour	3 cups	700 mL
Baking powder	1 tsp.	5 mL
Salt	½ tsp.	2 mL

Cream butter and sugar together. Add dry gelatin powder and mix. Beat in eggs 1 at a time.

Stir flour, baking powder and salt together and add. Mix well. Roll ¼ inch (6 mm) thick on lightly floured surface. Cut into 2 inch (5 cm) rounds. Arrange on greased baking sheet. Bake in 375°F (190°C) oven for 6 to 8 minutes. Makes 4 dozen.

Pictured on page 107.

CORKER BUNS

A lovely soft cookie to serve with tea. Not too rich.

Butter or margarine, softened	1 cup	250 mL
All-purpose flour	4 cups	1 L
Granulated sugar	1 cup	250 mL
Raisins	½ cup	125 mL
Baking powder	2 tsp.	10 mL
Salt	1 tsp.	5 mL
Boiling water	¾ cup	175 mL
Corn syrup	2 tsp.	10 mL
Eggs	2	2
Vanilla	1 tsp.	5 mL
Almond flavoring	1 tsp.	5 mL
Lemon flavoring	1 tsp.	5 mL

Rub butter and flour together until mealy.

Add sugar, raisins, baking powder and salt.

Measure water. Stir in corn syrup. Add to dry mixture.

Beat eggs and 3 flavorings together. Add and mix well. Drop by spoonfuls onto greased baking sheet. Bake in 350°F (180°C) oven for 12 to 15 minutes. Makes 5 dozen.

Pictured on page 107.

PEANUT BUTTER BALLS

These crispy-crunch balls are the best! Fabulous. My favorite.

Smooth peanut butter	1 cup	250 mL
Icing (confectioner's) sugar	1 cup	250 mL
Crisp rice cereal	1 cup	250 mL
Finely chopped walnuts	½ cup	125 mL
Butter or margarine, softened	1 tbsp.	15 mL
Semisweet chocolate squares	4 x 1 oz.	4 x 28 g
Grated parowax (paraffin)	2 tbsp.	30 mL

(continued on next page)

Measure first 5 ingredients into bowl. With your hands, mix together well. Shape into 1 inch (2.5 cm) balls. Chill for 2 to 3 hours.

Melt chocolate chips and wax together. Dip balls to coat, drain and place on waxed paper. Makes 4½ to 5 dozen.

SOUR CREAM SOFTIES

Mild in flavor, light in color. Soft and moist.

Butter or margarine	½ cup	125 mL
Granulated sugar	1½ cups	375 mL
Eggs	2	2
Vanilla	1 tsp.	5 mL
All-purpose flour	3 cups	750 mL
Salt	1 tsp.	5 mL
Baking powder	½ tsp.	2 mL
Baking soda	½ tsp.	2 mL
Sour cream	1 cup	250 mL
Brown sugar		
Cinnamon		

Cream butter and sugar together well. Beat in eggs 1 at a time. Add vanilla.

Mix flour, salt, baking powder and baking soda together.

Add flour mixture alternately with sour cream. Blend well to make a thick batter. Drop by 2 tbsp. (30 mL) quantity onto greased cookie sheet. Spread each into 2 inch (5 cm) circles.

Mix equal amounts of brown sugar and cinnamon together. Sprinkle over flattened cookies. Bake in 400°F (200°C) oven for about 8 to 12 minutes until golden around edges. Remove to rack to cool. Makes 3 dozen.

Pictured on page 107.

CHOCOLATE SOFTIES

Jazz these up with a bit of icing.

Butter or margarine, softened	½ cup	125 mL
Granulated sugar	1 cup	250 mL
Egg	1	1
Squares of unsweetened chocolate, melted	2 x 1 oz.	2 x 28 g
Sour milk	⅓ cup	75 mL
Vanilla	1 tsp.	5 mL
All-purpose flour	1¾ cups	400 mL
Baking soda	½ tsp.	2 mL
Salt	½ tsp.	2 mL
Chopped walnuts (optional)	½ cup	125 mL

Mix first 6 ingredients together well.

Stir in remaining ingredients. Drop by teaspoonfuls onto ungreased cookie sheet, allowing room for spreading. Bake in 400° F (200° C) oven for about 8 to 10 minutes. When pressed slightly, it should leave no dent. Remove from cookie sheet. Cool. Makes 4 dozen.

ICING

Icing (confectioner's) sugar	1¼ cups	300 mL
Cocoa	⅓ cup	75 mL
Butter or margarine, softened	3 tbsp.	45 mL
Hot coffee or water	5 tsp.	25 mL

Beat all together until smooth, adding a bit more liquid if needed to make proper spreading consistency. Ice cookies.

Pictured on page 107.

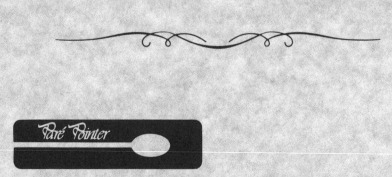

Paré Pointer

Would a sick crocodile be an illigator?

COCONUT LOGS

Like your favorite coconut chocolate bar. No baking.

Icing (confectioner's) sugar	2 cups	450 mL
Flaked coconut	2 cups	450 mL
Milk	2 tbsp.	30 mL
Butter or margarine, softened	1 tbsp.	15 mL
Semisweet chocolate chips	1 cup	250 mL
Grated parowax (paraffin)	3 tbsp.	50 mL

Mix first 4 ingredients together well. Shape into thumb size logs.

Melt chocolate chips and parowax in small saucepan over low heat. Dip logs in chocolate to cover. Drain and place on waxed paper. Makes 2½ dozen.

CARAMEL WAFERS

A caramely treat that suits any sweet tooth. Try it with soda crackers too.

Graham crackers		
Butter or margarine	1 cup	250 mL
Brown sugar, packed	¾ cup	175 mL
Flaked almonds	½ cup	125 mL

Line greased 10 x 15 inch (25 x 38 cm) pan with crackers.

Put butter and sugar into saucepan. Bring to boil stirring occasionally. Boil 3 minutes. Spoon evenly over crackers in pan.

Sprinkle almonds over top. Bake in 350°F (180°C) oven for 7 minutes. Cuts into 20 pieces.

Note: Chopped walnuts make a good substitute for almonds. More economical as well. Ground pecans are superb.

Paré Pointer

A jittery witch is better known as a twitch.

FRUIT ROCKS

A most attractive drop cookie with red cherries and nuts showing on top.

Butter or margarine	½ cup	125 mL
Brown sugar, packed	¾ cup	175 mL
Egg	1	1
Vanilla	1 tsp.	5 mL
All-purpose flour	1¼ cups	300 mL
Baking powder	½ tsp.	2 mL
Salt	½ tsp.	2 mL
Cinnamon	½ tsp.	2 mL
Chopped dates	1 cup	250 mL
Candied cherries, cut up	1 cup	250 mL
Candied pineapple ring, cut up	1	1
Chopped walnuts	½ cup	125 mL
Chopped almonds	½ cup	125 mL

Cream butter and sugar together well. Beat in egg and vanilla.

Add flour, baking powder, salt and cinnamon. Stir.

Add remaining ingredients. Mix together. Drop by teaspoonfuls onto greased cookie sheet. Bake in 325°F (160°C) oven for about 15 minutes. Makes about 7½ dozen.

FILBERT FINGERS

Dainty and elegant describe these scrumptious cookies. Pretty as a picture.

Butter (not margarine) softened	1 cup	250 mL
Brown sugar, packed	¾ cup	175 mL
All-purpose flour	2½ cups	625 mL
Milk	2 tbsp.	30 mL
Ground filberts	1 cup	250 mL
Semisweet chocolate squares	2 x 1 oz.	2 x 28 g
Grated parowax (paraffin)	2 tbsp.	30 mL

Mix butter, sugar, flour and milk together. Form into a ball and knead until soft and pliable.

Mix in nuts. Shape into fingers. Place on ungreased baking sheet. Bake in 375°F (190°C) oven for about 10 minutes. Cool.

Melt chocolate and parowax in saucepan over hot water. Dip ends of fingers. Place on waxed paper to set. Makes 6½ dozen.

CHOCOLATE NUGGETS

These are incredible cookies. They are extra rich and extra chocolaty and brownie-like. Make for a special treat when cost is no object.

Semisweet chocolate chips	2 cups	500 mL
Butter or margarine	¼ cup	60 mL
Sweetened condensed milk	11 oz.	300 mL
Granulated sugar	¼ cup	60 mL
Vanilla	1 tsp.	5 mL
All-purpose flour	1 cup	250 mL
Chopped nuts (optional)	½ cup	125 mL

Melt first 5 ingredients together in saucepan over medium heat. Stir often.

Add flour and nuts. Mix well. Drop by spoonfuls onto greased cookie sheet. Bake in 350°F (180°C) oven for about 10 to 12 minutes. Cookies will be soft. Makes 6 dozen.

OATMEAL CHIP COOKIES

Chocolate chips in a favorite oatmeal base produce the ultimate cookie. A great favorite.

Butter or margarine, softened	1 cup	250 mL
Brown sugar, packed	2 cups	500 mL
Eggs	2	2
Vanilla	1 tsp.	5 mL
All-purpose flour	2 cups	500 mL
Baking powder	1 tsp.	5 mL
Baking soda	½ tsp.	2 mL
Rolled oats	2 cups	500 mL
Semisweet chocolate chips	2 cups	500 mL
Medium coconut	¾ cup	175 mL

Cream butter and sugar together. Beat in eggs 1 at a time. Add vanilla.

Add remaining ingredients. Mix well. Drop by spoonfuls onto greased baking sheet. Bake in 350°F (180°C) oven for about 8 to 10 minutes. Makes 5 dozen.

OATMEAL CHIP PIZZA: Press 3 cups (750 mL) dough onto greased 12 inch (30 cm) pizza pan. Sprinkle with semisweet chocolate and butterscotch chips, nuts, coconut, candy coated chocolate (Smarties, M&M's) and any other treat you like. Allow a bit more time to bake.

CRACKERJACK COOKIES

Crunchy and good to please any age. A real crackerjack of a cookie.

Butter or margarine, softened	1 cup	250 mL
Brown sugar, packed	1 cup	250 mL
Granulated sugar	1 cup	250 mL
Eggs	2	2
Vanilla	2 tsp.	10 mL
Rolled oats	2 cups	500 mL
Crisp rice cereal	2 cups	500 mL
All-purpose flour	1½ cups	375 mL
Coconut	1 cup	250 mL
Baking powder	1 tsp.	5 mL
Baking soda	1 tsp.	5 mL

(continued on next page)

Mix first 5 ingredients together well.

Add remaining ingredients. Mix together. Shape into balls. Do not flatten. Arrange on ungreased baking sheet. Bake in 375°F (190°C) oven for 8 to 10 minutes. Makes about 6 dozen.

LEMON RAISIN COOKIES

It's a safe bet that you have never tasted a cookie so lemony and so good.

Raisins	1½ cups	375 mL
Water	1 cup	250 mL
Butter or margarine, softened	½ cup	125 mL
Brown sugar, packed	1¼ cups	175 mL
Egg	1	1
Grated rind of lemon	1	1
Lemon juice	2 tbsp.	30 mL
All-purpose flour	2 cups	500 mL
Baking powder	1 tsp.	5 mL
Baking soda	½ tsp.	2 mL
Salt	½ tsp.	2 mL
Chopped nuts	½ cup	125 mL

Bring raisins and water to a boil in saucepan. Remove from heat. Cool.

Cream butter, sugar and egg together. Add rind and juice.

Add remaining ingredients. Drain and add raisins to batter. Mix well. Drop by spoonfuls onto greased baking sheet. Bake in 375°F (190°C) oven for 8 to 10 minutes. Makes 3½ dozen.

Pictured on page 107.

Pare Pointer

Talk about stingy! First, doctors say they will treat you then they make you pay for it.

SLOW POKES

Baked long at a low temperature, these cookies shatter and melt in your mouth. A yummy caramel flavor.

Butter or margarine, softened	1 cup	250 mL
Granulated sugar	1 cup	250 mL
Egg yolk	1	1
Vanilla	2 tsp.	10 mL
All-purpose flour	2 cups	500 mL
Salt	¼ tsp.	1 mL
Baking powder	1 tsp.	5 mL
Hot water	2 tsp.	10 mL
Baking soda	1 tsp.	5 mL
Egg white	1	1
Finely chopped pecans or walnuts	½ cup	125 mL

Cream butter and sugar together. Add egg yolk and vanilla.

Mix in flour, salt and baking powder. Stir hot water and baking soda together and add. Mix well. Press thinly onto 2 ungreased baking sheets.

Beat egg white until frothy. Brush over top to glaze. Sprinkle with nuts. Bake in 250°F (120°C) oven for 1 hour. Cut into bars 1½ x 2½ inches (4 x 6.5 cm) as soon as they come from the oven. They will crumble if cut when cooled. Makes about 5 dozen.

Paré Pointer

When a dog barks at you, yet wags his tail, how do you know which end to believe?

SWEDISH TEA CAKES

You will need to double this recipe. Also known as Swedish Pastry and Thumbprints.

Butter or margarine, softened	½ cup	125 mL
Brown sugar, packed	¼ cup	50 mL
Egg yolk	1	1
All-purpose flour	1 cup	250 mL
Baking powder	½ tsp.	2 mL
Salt	⅛ tsp.	0.5 mL
Egg white, fork beaten	1	1
Finely chopped nuts for coating	⅔ cup	150 mL

Jam or jelly (red is best)

Cream butter and sugar together. Beat in egg yolk.

Stir flour, baking powder and salt together and add. Mix. Shape into small balls.

Dip into egg white, roll in nuts and place on greased baking sheet. Dent each with your thumb. Bake in 325°F (160°C) oven for 5 minutes. Remove and press dents again. Continue to bake for 10 to 15 minutes until golden brown.

Fill dents with jam while warm, or store unfilled to be filled as used. Makes about 20.

Paré Pointer

Please give up the idea of running away with the circus. The police will only make you bring it back.

SOFT MOLASSES DROPS

An old time recipe, these are moist and spicy.

All-purpose flour	3½ cups	800 mL
Granulated sugar	¾ cup	175 mL
Ginger	1 tsp.	5 mL
Cinnamon	1 tsp.	5 mL
Salt	½ tsp.	2 mL
Molasses	¾ cup	175 mL
Butter or margarine, softened	¾ cup	175 mL
Egg	1	1
Baking soda	1½ tsp.	7 mL
Hot coffee (or hot milk)	½ cup	125 mL

Measure first 8 ingredients in order given into mixing bowl.

Stir baking soda into hot coffee. Add and beat dough until thoroughly blended. Drop by tablespoonfuls onto greased cookie sheet. Bake in 375°F (190°C) oven for 10 to 12 minutes. Makes 5 dozen.

HERMITS

One of the best known drop cookies. Cookie jars are filled with these for after school snacks.

Butter or margarine, softened	1 cup	250 mL
Brown sugar, packed	1½ cups	375 mL
Eggs	3	3
Vanilla	1 tsp.	5 mL
All-purpose flour	3 cups	750 mL
Baking powder	1 tsp.	5 mL
Baking soda	1 tsp.	5 mL
Salt	½ tsp.	2 mL
Cinnamon	1 tsp.	5 mL
Nutmeg	½ tsp.	2 mL
Allspice	¼ tsp.	1 mL
Raisins	1 cup	250 mL
Chopped dates	1 cup	250 mL
Chopped nuts	⅔ cup	150 mL

(continued on next page)

Cream butter and sugar together. Beat in eggs 1 at a time. Add vanilla.

Measure in remaining ingredients. Mix well. Drop onto greased baking sheet by heaping teaspoonfuls. Bake in 375°F (190°C) oven for 6 to 8 minutes. Makes 4½ dozen.

PECAN BALLS

These tender little balls melt in your mouth. They are sometimes known as Mexican Wedding Cakes or Russian Tea Cakes.

Butter or margarine, softened	1 cup	250 mL
Icing (confectioner's) sugar	½ cup	125 mL
All-purpose flour	2¼ cups	550 mL
Ground pecans	1 cup	250 mL
Vanilla	2 tsp.	10 mL
Icing (confectioner's) sugar	½ cup	125 mL

Combine first 5 ingredients in bowl. Mix first with spoon then by hand to work it until it holds together. Shape into 1 inch (2.5 cm) balls. Arrange on ungreased baking sheet. Bake in 325°F (160°C) oven for 20 to 25 minutes.

As soon as balls have cooled enough to handle, roll them in icing sugar. Makes about 6 dozen.

ALMOND BALLS: Omit pecans. Add 1 cup (250 mL) ground almonds.

ALMOND CRESCENTS: Omit pecans. Add 2 cups (500 mL) ground almonds. Roll into ropes as thick as your finger. Cut into 2 inch (5 cm) lengths. Pinch ends to taper. Shape into crescents.

BURIED CHERRY: Completely cover well drained maraschino cherries with dough. Bake same as above.

Paré Pointer

It is difficult to understand twin doctors. They are a pair-a-docs.

SHORTBREAD

So delicate! Keep a supply in the freezer. It thaws quickly.

Butter (not margarine) softened	1 lb.	454 g
Sugar, use half brown and half icing (confectioner's) sugar	¾ cup	175 mL
All-purpose flour	4 cups	900 mL
Red and green sugar, mixed		
Candied cherries, cut up		

Mix butter, sugar and flour together well. With your hands, squeeze and work until it will hold together. Make 4 rolls about 1½ inches (3.5 cm) in diameter. May be sliced and baked at this point but makes a much rounder cookie if chilled first. May be chilled overnight or just an hour or two. Slice ¼ inch (1.1 cm) thick. Arrange on ungreased baking sheet.

Sprinkle some cookies with sugar. Lightly push piece of cherry into center of some others. Bake at 325°F (160°C) oven for about 15 to 20 minutes or until lightly browned around edges. Remove from baking sheet to counter top. Makes about 6 dozen.

Note: For a whiter shortbread use all icing sugar instead of part brown sugar. May also be rolled on lightly floured surface and cut into shapes.

KRUNCHY KRISPS

Crispy and crunchy. A good cookie jar filler.

Butter or margarine, softened	1 cup	250 mL
Granulated sugar	¾ cup	175 mL
Brown sugar, packed	¾ cup	175 mL
Eggs	2	2
Vanilla	1 tsp.	5 mL
All-purpose flour	1½ cups	375 mL
Rolled oats	1½ cups	375 mL
Coconut	½ cup	125 mL
Cinnamon	1 tsp.	5 mL
Baking powder	1 tsp.	5 mL
Baking soda	½ tsp.	2 mL

(continued on next page)

Cream butter and both sugars together in mixing bowl. Beat in eggs and vanilla.

Stir in remaining ingredients. Drop by spoonfuls onto lightly greased cookie sheet. Bake in 375°F (190°C) oven for about 10 minutes until browned. Makes about 5 dozen.

RAINBOW CHIP COOKIES

These delicious cookies contain no flour. Soft and chewy with candy-coated chocolate added. Makes a huge batch.

Smooth peanut butter	6 cups	1.3 L
Butter or margarine, softened	2 cups	500 mL
Brown sugar, packed	6 cups	1.3 L
Granulated sugar	4 cups	1 L
Eggs	12	12
Vanilla	1 tbsp.	15 mL
Corn syrup	1 tbsp.	15 mL
Rolled oats	18 cups	4 L
Baking soda	8 tsp.	40 mL
Semisweet chocolate chips	2 cups	450 mL
Candy-coated chocolate bits, such as Smarties & M&M's	2 cups	450 mL

In mixing bowl, cream peanut butter, butter, brown and granulated sugar together. Beat in eggs, 2 at a time. Mix in vanilla and syrup. Transfer to extra large container.

Mix in remaining ingredients. Drop by ice cream scoop onto greased pan. Flatten with hand. May be dropped by teaspoonfuls for a smaller cookie. Bake in 350°F (180°C) oven for 10 to 12 minutes for large cookies and 7 to 8 minutes for small. Overbaking makes them hard. Makes 5 dozen, 3 inch (8 cm) cookies, 1 dozen, 5 inch (13 cm) cookies and 1 pizza cookie.

PIZZA: Use 3 cups (700 mL) cookie dough. Press into greased 12 inch (30 cm) pizza pan. Sprinkle with more semisweet chocolate chips, butterscotch chips, Smarties or M&M's, cereal flakes, coconut, peanuts and any other things you fancy. Bake for 12 to 15 minutes. Serve in wedges, warm or cold.

RAISIN FILLED COOKIES

Serve hot from the oven for an extra special delight. Dough and filling can be kept refrigerated to bake as needed if desired.

FILLING

Raisins, coarsely chopped	1½ cups	375 mL
Granulated sugar	¾ cup	175 mL
Cornstarch	1 tbsp.	15 mL
Water	¾ cup	175 mL
Lemon juice	1½ tsp.	7 mL

COOKIE DOUGH

Butter or margarine, softened	1 cup	250 mL
Granulated sugar	1½ cups	375 mL
Eggs	2	2
Milk	½ cup	125 mL
Vanilla	1 tsp.	5 mL
All-purpose flour	3½ cups	875 mL
Baking soda	1 tsp.	5 mL
Salt	½ tsp.	2 mL

Granulated sugar for garnish

Filling: Mix all ingredients together in saucepan. Bring to a boil, stirring over medium heat. Cool.

Cookie Dough: Cream butter and sugar together. Beat in eggs 1 at a time. Add milk and vanilla.

Stir flour, baking soda and salt together and add. Mix well. Roll out thinly on floured surface. Cut into 2½ inch (6.5 cm) circles. Arrange circles on greased baking sheet. Drop 1 tsp. (5 mL) raisin filling in center. Cover with second circle. Press edges with floured fork.

Cut a cross in top center about ½ to ¾ inch (1.25 to 2 cm) each way.

Sprinkle with sugar. Bake in 350°F (180°C) oven until lightly browned, about 10 minutes. Makes 4 dozen.

Paré Pointer

She knows that a briefcase is a short law suit.

CHOCOLATE PINEAPPLE DESSERT

The hint of pineapple is complemented by the chocolate crust. Refreshing.

CRUST

Butter or margarine	½ cup	125 mL
Graham cracker crumbs	2 cups	500 mL
Granulated sugar	¼ cup	50 mL
Cocoa	¼ cup	50 mL

FILLING

Unflavored gelatin powder	¼ oz.	7 g
Cold water	⅓ cup	75 mL
Boiling water	⅓ cup	75 mL
Juice of lemon	1	1
Salt	⅛ tsp.	0.5 mL
Eggs whites, beaten stiff	3	3
(optional — gives more volume)		
Granulated sugar	½ cup	125 mL
Vanilla	½ tsp.	2 mL
Crushed pineapple, drained well	14 oz.	398 mL
Whipping cream (or 1 env. topping)	1 cup	250 mL

Crust: Melt butter in medium saucepan over medium heat. Stir in crumbs, sugar and cocoa. Measure ½ cup (125 mL) for topping. Press remaining crumbs into ungreased 9 x 13 inch (22 x 33 cm) pan.

Filling: Sprinkle gelatin over cold water in small saucepan. Let stand for 5 minutes.

Add boiling water, lemon juice and salt. Heat, stirring, over medium heat until dissolved. Chill until syrupy.

Fold in egg whites (if using), sugar, vanilla and pineapple.

Whip cream until stiff. Fold in. Pour over chocolate crust. Smooth top. Scatter reserved crumbs over all. Chill. Cuts into 12 or 15 pieces.

Little Susie thought a cold pop was an Eskimo's father.

PINEAPPLE DELIGHT

Although this is an extra-special favorite, be sure to try the strawberry variation. So showy. So good.

CRUST

Butter or margarine	½ cup	125 mL
Graham cracker crumbs	2 cups	500 mL
Granulated sugar	¼ cup	50 mL

FILLING

Icing (confectioner's) sugar	1½ cups	375 mL
Butter or margarine, softened	½ cup	125 mL
Eggs	2	2
Crushed pineapple, drained	19 oz.	540 mL
Whipping cream (or 1 env. topping)	1 cup	250 mL

Crust: Melt butter in saucepan over medium heat. Stir in crumbs and sugar. Reserve 1 cup (250 mL) for topping. Press remaining crumbs into ungreased 9 x 13 inch (22 x 33 cm) pan. Bake in 350°F (180°C) oven for 10 minutes. Cool.

Filling: Beat icing sugar and butter together well. Add eggs, 1 at a time, beating until smooth. Spread over crumb layer.

Scatter pineapple over top. Whip cream until stiff. Spread over pineapple. Pineapple may be folded into cream, if desired, before spreading. Sprinkle with reserved crumbs. Cuts into 15 pieces.

STRAWBERRY DELIGHT: Omit pineapple. Drain juice from 15 oz. (425 g) frozen sliced strawberries. Stir in 1 tbsp. (15 mL) cornstarch. Heat and stir until boiling and thickened. Cool. Stir in berries and use in place of pineapple. Makes a pretty red layer and is delicious.

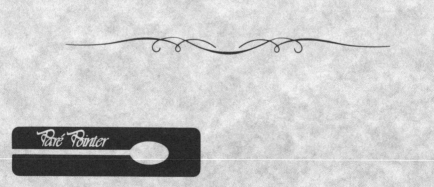

Paré Pointer

Sheep are destined to be poor. They are always being fleeced.

This version is quick and easy without sacrificing flavor. Impress your friends.

Dark chocolate cake layers, 8 or 9 inch (20 or 23 cm) round	2	2
Kirsch — a generous sprinkling (or sherry or fruit juice)		
Icing (confectioner's) sugar	1 cup	250 mL
Cocoa	2 tbsp.	30 mL
Butter or margarine	2 tbsp.	30 mL
Prepared coffee or water	1 tbsp.	15 mL
Can of cherry pie filling	19 oz.	540 mL
Whipping cream (or 1½ env. topping)	1½ cups	375 mL
Granulated sugar	4 tsp.	20 mL
Vanilla	1 tsp.	5 mL

First make icing. Beat icing sugar, cocoa, butter and coffee or water together adding a bit more liquid if needed.

To assemble cake, put 1 layer on cake plate, rounded side down. Sprinkle generously with kirsch. Apply ½ of chocolate icing to top of layer on the outside edge only, forming a rim about ½ inch (1.25 cm) high and ¾ inch (2 cm) wide. Spread ½ can cherry pie filling over layer keeping it inside of icing rim. Put second layer, flat side down, over top. Sprinkle with kirsch. Cut rounded top off if needed to make top flat enough so that cherries will stay in place. Make another icing rim. Spread second ½ can cherry pie filling over top, keeping inside of rim.

Whip cream, sugar and vanilla until stiff. Using rubber spatula, ice sides of cake with whipped cream. Pile rest of cream on top center of cake. Spread almost to edge of cherries so some cherries may still be seen or leave some center cherries showing and spread cream around the top edges. Top with stemmed cherries and/or chocolate curls to make it extra special. Slice into 12 generous portions.

Variation: Canned black cherries, pitted, may be used. Thicken juice of 2 x 14 oz. (2 x 398 mL) cans with 2 tbsp. (30 mL) cornstarch stirred into juice, then heat and stir to boil and thicken.

BLACK FOREST BOWL: Partly fill bowl with chunks of chocolate cake. Spoon cherry pie filling over top. Put sweetened whipped cream over all. Garnish with shaved chocolate and cherries. Chill.

PIE CRUST PASTRY

For pies, quiches, meat pies and sausage rolls. Makes a tender, flaky pie crust.

All-purpose flour	5 cups	1.1 L
Salt	2 tsp.	10 mL
Baking powder	1 tsp.	5 mL
Brown sugar	3 tbsp.	45 mL
Lard, room temperature	1 lb.	454 g
Egg	1	1
Vinegar	2 tbsp.	30 mL
Add cold water to make	1 cup	225 mL

Measure flour, salt, baking powder and brown sugar into large bowl. Stir together to distribute all ingredients.

Add lard. Cut into pieces with knife. With pastry cutter, cut in lard until whole mixture is crumbly and feels moist.

Break egg into measuring cup. Fork beat well. Add vinegar. Add cold water to measure 1 cup (225 mL). Pour slowly over flour mixture stirring with fork to distribute. With hands, work until it will hold together. Divide into 4 equal parts. Each part is sufficient for a 2-crust pie. Wrap in plastic and store in refrigerator for 1 or 2 weeks. Store in freezer to have a continuing supply.

FRUIT PIZZA

Make your own color arrangement. A sight to behold.

CRUST		
All-purpose flour	1¼ cups	275 mL
Brown sugar	⅓ cup	75 mL
Icing (confectioner's) sugar	3 tbsp.	50 mL
Butter, softened	⅔ cup	150 mL
TOPPING		
Cream cheese, softened	12 oz.	375 g
Granulated sugar	½ cup	125 mL
Vanilla	1 tsp.	5 mL
Variety of fruit		

(continued on next page)

Crust: Mix all 4 ingredients together in bowl until it forms a ball. Press into bottom of 12 inch (30 cm) pizza pan. Bake in 350° F (180° C) oven for about 10 to 15 minutes or until golden brown. Cool.

Topping: Beat cheese, sugar and vanilla together. Spread over crust. Arrange fruit in pattern of your choice over top. Glaze fruit.

APRICOT GLAZE: Mix ¼ cup (60 mL) apricot jam or orange marmalade with 1 tbsp. (30 mL) water. Rub through sieve.

YOGURT POUND CAKE

You will love the texture of this tasty cake. Use as a coffeecake or dessert.

Egg whites, room temperature	6	6
Cream of tartar	¼ tsp.	1 mL
Granulated sugar	½ cup	125 mL
Butter or margarine, softened	1 cup	250 mL
Granulated sugar	1½ cups	375 mL
Eggs yolks	6	6
Grated lemon rind	2 tsp.	10 mL
Lemon juice	2 tbsp.	30 mL
All-purpose flour	3 cups	750 mL
Baking soda	1 tsp.	5 mL
Salt	¼ tsp.	1 mL
Unflavored yogurt	1 cup	250 mL

Beat egg whites with cream of tartar until soft peaks form. Add first amount of sugar gradually, beating continually, until mixture is stiff and glossy. Set aside.

Cream butter and second amount of sugar. Beat in egg yolks 1 at a time. Mix in lemon rind and juice.

Add flour, baking soda and salt alternately with yogurt. Beat until smooth after each addition.

Gently fold egg whites into batter. Pour into a greased and floured 10 inch (25 cm) tube pan. Bake in 350°F (180°C) oven for about 1 hour. Cool. Remove from pan by loosening sides with knife. Invert on plate. Dust with icing (confectioner's) sugar before serving.

SAUCY FUDGE PUDDING

The fudge batter rises to the top as it bakes, leaving a rich chocolate sauce beneath.

All-purpose flour	1 cup	250 mL
Granulated sugar	¾ cup	175 mL
Cocoa	2 tbsp.	30 mL
Baking powder	2 tsp.	10 mL
Salt	¼ tsp.	1 mL
Milk	½ cup	125 mL
Cooking oil (or butter, melted)	2 tbsp.	30 mL
Chopped nuts, optional	½ cup	125 mL
Brown sugar, packed	¾ cup	175 mL
Cocoa	2 tbsp.	30 mL
Hot water	1¾ cup	425 mL

Measure flour, sugar, cocoa, baking powder and salt into bowl. Stir. Add milk, oil and nuts, if you are using them. Mix together with spoon and scrape into 8 inch (20 cm) casserole or pan.

In same bowl mix sugar and cocoa together. Add water. Stir to dissolve sugar. Pour over batter but do not stir. Bake, uncovered, in 350°F (180°C) oven for about 40 minutes until batter has risen above sauce and is firm to touch. Serves 6.

1. Orange Cheesecake page 138
2. Raspberry Cheesecake page 140
3. Raspberry Sauce page 135
4. Ginger Cream Dessert page 128

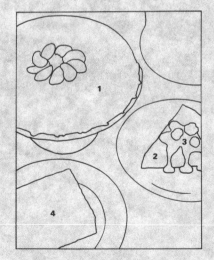

LEMON CHIFFON CHEESECAKE

A frothy delicate delight both to the eye and the palate. A no-bake wonder.

CRUST

Butter or margarine	¼ cup	50 mL
Graham cracker crumbs	1¼ cups	300 mL
Granulated sugar	2 tbsp.	30 mL

FILLING

Unflavored gelatin	2 x ¼ oz.	2 x 7 g
Cold water	½ cup	125 mL
Egg yolks	2	2
Milk	½ cup	125 mL
Granulated sugar	1 cup	250 mL
Salt	1 tsp.	5 mL
Creamed cottage cheese, blender smoothed (or sieved)	2 cups	500 mL
Grated rind and juice of lemon	1	1
Lemon juice	2 tbsp.	30 mL
Vanilla	1 tsp.	5 mL
Egg whites	2	2
Whipping cream (or 1 env. topping)	1 cup	250 mL

Crust: Melt butter in saucepan. Add crumbs and sugar. Stir to mix. Pack into bottom and sides of ungreased 9 inch (22 cm) springform or 8 x 8 inch (20 x 20 cm) pan. Chill.

Filling: Sprinkle gelatin over water in top of double boiler. Let stand 5 minutes. Place over boiling water.

Add yolks and beat with spoon. Stir in milk, sugar and salt. Heat and stir over hot water until gelatin and sugar are dissolved. Chill until syrupy.

Fold cottage cheese, rind, lemon juice and vanilla into thickening gelatin.

Whip egg whites until stiff, then using same beater, beat cream until stiff. Fold in egg whites, then fold in whipped cream. Pour over crumbs. Chill. Serve with your favorite pudding sauce. Serves 12.

GINGER CREAM DESSERT

A fluffy light treat. Add or subtract ginger to suit your fancy.

FIRST LAYER

Butter or margarine	¼ cup	60 mL
Ginger snap crumbs	1 cup	250 mL

SECOND LAYER

Unflavored gelatin powder	¼ oz.	7 g
Water	¼ cup	50 mL
Whipping cream (or 1 env. topping)	1 cup	250 mL
Crushed pineapple, drained	14 oz.	398 mL
Ginger marmalade or crabapple jelly	1 tbsp.	15 mL
Ginger	1 tsp.	5 mL
Ginger snap crumbs for garnish	2 tbsp.	30 mL

First Layer: Melt butter in small saucepan. Stir in first amount of crumbs. Press into ungreased 8 x 8 inch (20 x 20 cm) pan. Chill.

Second Layer: Sprinkle gelatin over water in small saucepan. Let stand 5 minutes. Heat to dissolve. Cool until syrupy.

Whip cream until stiff. Beat in gelatin. Fold in pineapple, marmalade and ginger. Pour over first layer.

Scatter remaining crumbs over top. Chill. Serves 9.

Pictured on page 125.

AFTER DINNER MINTS

What could make a better ending than your own soft delicately-flavored, delicately-colored mints?

Icing (confectioner's) sugar	2½ cups	600 mL
Butter or margarine, softened	3 tbsp.	50 mL
Cream	2 tbsp.	30 mL
Peppermint flavoring	½ tsp.	2 mL
Food coloring		

(continued on next page)

Mix all ingredients together well. Dough should be fairly stiff but still pliable enough to roll. Add a bit more icing sugar or cream as needed for right consistency. Divide into separate chunks to tint different colors. Leave 1 chunk plain. Roll into rope about ½ inch (1.5 cm) in diameter. Cut into pieces. Let stand on waxed paper several hours, at least overnight. Makes several dozen mints. May also be pressed into candy molds.

Pictured on page 53.

STRAWBERRY FREEZE

A remarkable dessert. Cuts easily and can be served immediately. Keep it on hand. A pretty pink color.

CRUST

Butter or margarine	¾ cup	175 mL
All-purpose flour	1½ cups	375 mL
Brown sugar, packed	½ cup	125 mL
Finely chopped nuts	¾ cup	175 mL
FILLING		
Egg whites	2	2
Granulated sugar	¾ cup	175 mL
Frozen sliced strawberries, partly thawed	15 oz.	425 g
Lemon juice	2 tbsp.	30 mL
Whipping cream (or 1 env. topping)	1 cup	250 mL

Crust: Melt butter in medium size saucepan. Stir in flour, sugar and nuts. Spread in large ungreased baking pan. Bake in 375°F (190°C) oven for 15 to 20 minutes, stirring twice, until nicely browned. Remove from oven. Break up any chunks. Scatter ⅔ crumbs into ungreased 9 x 13 inch (23 x 33 cm) pan or 10 inch (25 cm) springform pan.

Filling: In large mixing bowl put egg whites, sugar, strawberries and lemon juice. Beat on high speed until thickened and volume is increased. This will take about 10 minutes.

Beat cream until stiff. Fold into strawberry mixture. Turn into crumb-lined pan. Sprinkle reserved crumbs over top. Cover and freeze overnight or until needed. After first piece is removed, use egg lifter (turner) to take out rest. Serves 12 to 15.

CHERRY CHEESECAKE

A dessert lover's glistening special.

CRUST

Butter or margarine	½ cup	125 mL
Graham cracker crumbs	1½ cups	375 mL

FILLING

Cream cheese, softened	8 oz.	250 g
Granulated sugar	1 cup	250 mL
Lemon juice	1 tbsp.	15 mL
Whipping cream (or 1 env. topping)	1 cup	250 mL
Milk	½ cup	125 mL
Cherry pie filling	19 oz.	540 mL

Crust: Melt butter in saucepan over medium heat. Stir in crumbs. Press into 9 x 9 inch (22 x 22 cm) pan. Bake in 350° F (180° C) oven for 10 minutes. Cool.

Filling: Beat cheese, sugar and lemon juice together to dissolve sugar.

Whip cream until stiff. Fold into cheese mixture and spread over base. Chill.

Spread cherry filling over top. Chill. Serves 9.

BLUEBERRY CHEESECAKE: Use blueberry pie filling instead of cherry.

LEMON SAUCED PUDDING

As the batter cooks, it rises to the top. Makes a light pudding with lemon sauce to spoon over top.

Egg whites	2	2
Butter or margarine, softened	1 tbsp.	15 mL
Granulated sugar	1 cup	225 mL
All-purpose flour	¼ cup	50 mL
Egg yolks	2	2
Lemon, juice and grated rind	1	1
Salt	⅛ tsp.	0.5 mL
Milk	1½ cups	350 mL

(continued on next page)

Beat egg whites in small bowl until stiff. Set aside.

Measure butter, sugar, flour, egg yolks, lemon juice, rind, salt and milk into mixing bowl. Beat lightly until blended. Fold in beaten egg whites. Turn into 8 inch (20 cm) casserole. Set in pan of hot water and bake in 350°F (180°C) oven for about 45 minutes until browned. Makes 6 servings.

LAZY DAISY CAKE

A white sponge-type cake that is iced, then caramelized in the oven. Great flavor. Easy to make from scratch.

Eggs	2	2
Granulated sugar	1 cup	250 mL
Vanilla	1 tsp.	5 mL
All-purpose flour	1 cup	250 mL
Baking powder	1 tsp.	5 mL
Salt	¼ tsp.	1 mL
Milk, heated	½ cup	125 mL
Butter or margarine	1 tbsp.	15 mL

Beat eggs in mixing bowl until frothy. Beat in sugar in 4 or 5 separate additions. Stir in vanilla.

Stir in flour, baking powder and salt.

Heat milk and butter together in small saucepan until hot. Add, stirring carefully. Scrape into greased 9 x 9 inch (22 x 22 cm) pan. Bake in 350° F (180° C) oven about 25 minutes, until it tests done with toothpick. Put on topping.

TOPPING		
Brown sugar, packed	⅔ cup	150 mL
Butter or margarine	¼ cup	50 mL
Cream or milk	2 tbsp.	30 mL
Coconut	½ cup	125 mL

Combine all ingredients together in small saucepan. Heat and stir until hot and sugar is dissolved. Spread over cake. Return to oven until it bubbles well, about 3 to 5 minutes.

Variation: An equal amount of chopped nuts may be substituted for the coconut if preferred.

LEMON JELLY DESSERT

A light dessert, sort of like a cheesecake without any cheese. Slight lemon flavor. Just right after a heavy meal.

CRUST
Graham cracker crumbs, good sprinkle

FILLING

Lemon flavored gelatin	3 oz.	85 g
Boiling water	1 cup	250 mL
Cold water	½ cup	100 mL
Evaporated milk, freezer chilled	14 oz.	385 mL
Granulated sugar	1 cup	250 mL
Juice of lemon	1	1

Graham cracker crumbs, good sprinkle

Crust: Sprinkle crumbs, to cover, over bottom of ungreased 9 x 9 inch (22 x 22 cm) pan or if you would like more not-so-deep servings use 9 x 13 inch (22 x 33 cm) pan.

Filling: Stir gelatin with boiling water to dissolve. Add cold water. Chill until syrupy.

Beat partially frozen milk until soft peaks form. Add sugar and lemon juice. Beat again until quite stiff. Beat in thickened jelly. Carefully pour filling over crumbs. Smooth top.

Sprinkle crumbs over top. Chill. Serves 9 generously.

PEACH FLUFF

An exceptionally light smooth dessert. Even after the heaviest meal you will have room for this delicate dish.

Peach flavored gelatin	3 oz.	85 mL
Vanilla pudding and pie filling (not instant), 4 serving size	1	1
Water	2½ cups	750 mL
Whipping cream (or 1 env. topping)	1 cup	250 mL
Sliced peaches	1 cup	250 mL

(continued on next page)

Put first 3 ingredients into saucepan. Stir well. Bring to a boil, stirring frequently. Chill until syrupy.

Whip cream until stiff. Fold into thickened jelly mixture. Pour into pretty bowl. Chill.

Serve, topped with peaches. If using canned peaches, use juice to replace some of the water. Serves 6.

Pictured on page 143.

BROWN BETTY

An all time favorite. Good hot or cold.

Cooking apples, peeled and sliced	6 cups	1.5 L
Granulated sugar	¾ cup	175 mL
TOPPING		
All-purpose flour	1¾ cups	300 mL
Brown sugar, packed	¾ cup	175 mL
Butter or margarine	½ cup	125 mL
Salt	½ tsp.	2 mL

Fill 10 inch (25 cm) round casserole with apples about 2 to 3 inches deep. Pour granulated sugar over top.

Topping: Mix flour, brown sugar, butter and salt until crumbly. Scatter over sugared apples. Pat down lightly with hand. Bake, uncovered, in 375°F (190°C) oven for about 40 minutes until apples are tender. Serve with whipped cream or ice cream. Serves 8 generously.

RHUBARB BETTY: Use sliced fresh or frozen rhubarb, instead of apple, with a touch more sugar. Better yet, add a few raisins and omit the extra sugar. Equally as good.

FRESH FRUIT BETTY: Use fresh peaches, peeled and sliced, or fresh apricots, quartered, instead of apple.

DEEP APPLE: Sprinkle apples with cinnamon. Cover with pastry. Cut slits in top. Sprinkle with a bit of granulated sugar. Bake as above.

CHOCOLATE CHERRIES

You will get rave reviews when you serve these with coffee. Chocolate covers a peanut butter coating.

Maraschino cherries with stems, drained overnight	40 - 50	40 - 50
Smooth peanut butter	1 cup	250 mL
Icing (confectioner's) sugar	1 cup	250 mL
Butter or margarine, softened	2 tbsp.	30 mL
Semisweet chocolate squares	8	8
Grated parowax (paraffin)	¾ cup	175 mL

Have cherries very well drained and dry on paper towels overnight.

Mix peanut butter, icing sugar and butter together well. Cover each cherry with a thin coat. If it is too thick, chocolate won't cling very well.

Melt chocolate and parowax in pan over hot water. Dip cherries into warm mixture. If chocolate is too hot it won't cling to covered cherry. Place on waxed paper. Store in covered container. These keep for weeks. Makes 40 to 50.

Note: Semisweet chocolate chips may be used — 1⅓ cups (300 mL).

Pictured on page 143.

SIX LAYER CAKE

An easy company dessert. Good hot or cold. Serve hot with ice cream or cold with whipped cream. A pudding type cake.

Crushed pineapple with juice	14 oz.	398 mL
Cherry pie filling	19 oz.	540 mL
Yellow cake mix, 2 layer size	1	1
Butter or margarine, melted	¾ cup	175 mL
Flaked coconut	3 cups	750 mL
Chopped pecans or walnuts	1 cup	250 mL

Spread pineapple in greased 9 x 13 inch (22 x 33 cm) pan. Spoon pie filling over top. Sprinkle dry cake mix over pie filling. Drizzle melted butter over cake. Scatter coconut over top followed by nuts. Bake in 325°F (160°C) oven for about 1 hour 15 minutes until browned. Serves 15 to 18.

Smooth as satin crowned with a raspberry sauce. Gorgeous!

Unflavored gelatin powder	3 × ¼ oz.	3 × 7 g
Water	¾ cup	175 mL
Granulated sugar	1 cup	250 mL
Cream cheese, softened	8 oz.	250 g
Sour cream	2 cups	500 mL
Heavy cream	2 cups	500 mL
Vanilla	½ tsp.	2 mL

Sprinkle gelatin over water in small saucepan. Let stand 5 minutes. Heat and stir to dissolve. Remove from heat.

Beat sugar and cream cheese together well. Add gelatin and beat together.

Beat in sour cream, heavy cream and vanilla. Pour into 4 cup (1 L) mold. Chill.

Pictured on front cover.

RASPBERRY SAUCE

Fresh raspberries	1 cup	250 mL
Granulated sugar	¼ cup	60 mL
Water	⅓ cup	75 mL
Cornstarch	4 tsp.	20 mL
Fresh raspberries	1 cup	250 mL

Mash first amount of raspberries with sugar. Put into saucepan. Bring to boil over medium heat.

Measure water. Mix in cornstarch. Stir into mashed berries until thickened. Remove from heat. Rub through sieve to remove seeds. Cool thoroughly. Drizzle over unmolded dessert.

Arrange remaining whole raspberries on top and around sides.

Pictured on front cover and page 125.

CHOCOLATE LEAVES: Wipe leaves with wet cloth. Blot with paper towel. Dip shiny sides (tops) into melted semisweet chocolate. Chill until firm. Peel off.

Pictured on front cover.

Note: For a lighter dessert replace heavy cream with the same amount of milk.

CHERRY CHA CHA

A dessert that requires second helpings. The red cherry filling sandwiched between marshmallow cream and topped with rich crumbs makes it colorful.

CRUST

Butter or margarine	½ cup	125 mL
Graham cracker crumbs	2 cups	500 mL
Granulated sugar	¼ cup	50 mL

FILLING

Whipping cream (or 2 env. topping)	2 cups	500 mL
Tiny white marshmallows	4 cups	1 L
Cherry pie filling	19 oz.	540 mL

Crust: Melt butter in saucepan over medium heat. Stir in crumbs and sugar. Reserve ⅓ for topping. Press remaining crumbs in ungreased 9 x 13 inch (22 x 33 cm) pan. Bake in 350°F (180°C) oven for 10 minutes. Cool. This works well without baking too.

Filling: Whip cream until stiff. Fold in marshmallows. Spread ½ of this over crumb base.

Spoon cherry pie filling, a small amount at a time, over top, smoothing as well as you can. Spread second ½ cream mixture over pie filling. Sprinkle reserved crumbs over all. Chill for several hours before using. Cuts into 12 pieces.

CHOCOLATE STRAWBERRY SHORTCAKE

At last! A shortcake for chocolate lovers.

Chocolate cake layers 8 or 9 inch (20 or 22 cm) your own or a mix	2	2
Fresh strawberries	4 cups	1 L
Granulated sugar to taste		
Whipping cream (or 2 env. topping)	2 cups	500 mL
Granulated sugar	2 tbsp.	30 mL
Vanilla	2 tsp.	10 mL

(continued on next page)

Put 1 cake layer rounded side down on plate. Mash strawberries with sugar to taste (or slice) keeping some whole berries for garnish. Spread ½ mashed berries over bottom layer.

Beat cream with sugar and vanilla until stiff. Smooth ½ cream over berries. Place second cake layer smooth side down over cream.

Spoon remaining mashed berries over top of cake. Cover with remaining whipped cream. Slice whole berries and garnish as in photo. For the finishing touch dip a few slices in melted semisweet chocolate.

Pictured on page 143.

PINEAPPLE CREAM CAKE

Makes a light and easy dessert, sort of like trifle in a pan.

Cake mix, 2 layer size, white or yellow	1	1
Crushed pineapple	19 oz.	540 mL
Icing (confectioner's) sugar	½ cup	125 mL
Cornstarch	1 tbsp.	15 mL
Instant vanilla pudding, 4 serving size, prepared	1	1
Whipping cream	1 cup	250 mL
Sliced almonds	⅓ cup	75 mL

Prepare and bake cake mix as directed on package in 9 x 13 inch (22 x 33 cm) pan.

In saucepan stir pineapple, sugar and cornstarch together. Heat and stir until it boils and thickens. Spread on warm cake.

Prepare instant pudding as directed on package. Spoon over top of pineapple.

Whip cream until stiff. Spoon over pudding. Smooth.

Sprinkle with almonds. Cuts into 15 or 18 pieces.

ORANGE CHEESECAKE

An especially light and delicate dessert. Contains cottage cheese. Only the crust is baked.

FIRST LAYER

Butter or margarine	6 tbsp.	100 mL
Graham cracker crumbs	1¼ cups	300 mL
Granulated sugar	⅓ cup	75 mL

SECOND LAYER

Orange flavored gelatin	3 oz.	85 g
Boiling water	1 cup	250 mL
Juice drained from oranges plus water if needed	1 cup	200 mL
Cottage cheese, sieved	1 cup	250 mL
Whipping cream (or 1 env. topping)	1 cup	250 mL

THIRD LAYER

Canned mandarin oranges, drained	10 oz.	284 mL

GLAZE

Granulated sugar	¼ cup	50 mL
Water	¼ cup	50 mL
Cornstarch	1½ tsp.	7 mL

First Layer: Melt butter in saucepan. Stir in crumbs and sugar. Pack into ungreased 8 inch (20 cm) springform pan. Bake in 350°F (180°C) oven for 10 minutes. Cool.

Second Layer: Dissolve gelatin in boiling water. Stir in juice. Chill until syrupy.

Fold sieved cottage cheese into thickened jelly.

Whip cream until stiff. Fold into mixture. Pour into prepared pan. Chill.

Third Layer: Blot oranges dry with paper towels. Arrange over top of cheesecake. May be served as is but glaze adds to the appearance.

Glaze: Mix all ingredients together in saucepan. Bring to boil, stirring to thicken. Cool. Brush oranges to seal and shine. Serves 8.

Pictured on page 125.

HAZELNUT TORTE

This mysterious dessert triples in thickness as it cooks. Rich, nutty flavor. For three layers make one and one half times the recipe.

CAKE

Eggs	4	4
Granulated sugar	¾ cup	175 mL
All-purpose flour	2 tbsp.	30 mL
Baking powder	2½ tsp.	12 mL
Hazelnuts	1 cup	250 mL

FILLING

Butter or margarine, softened	2 tbsp.	30 mL
Icing (confectioner's) sugar	1 cup	225 mL
Cocoa	1 tsp.	5 mL
Vanilla	½ tsp.	2 mL
Boiling water	2 tbsp.	30 mL
Instant coffee granules	½ tsp.	2 mL

TOPPING

Whipping cream (or 1 env. topping)	1 cup	250 mL
Granulated sugar	1 tbsp.	15 mL
Vanilla	½ tsp.	2 mL

Chocolate shavings

Cake: Put first 5 ingredients into blender. Blend for 3 minutes. Scrape sides down once or twice during blending. Grease bottoms only of two 8 or 9 inch (20 or 22 cm) round pans. Pour batter into pans, being sure it is level and touches all sides. Bake in 350°F (180°C) oven for 20 minutes. Cool.

Filling: In small bowl beat butter, icing sugar, cocoa and vanilla together.

Mix water and coffee granules to dissolve. Add and beat. Run knife around edges of cake pans. Place 1 layer top side up on plate. Smooth filling over top. Cover with second layer, top side up.

Topping: Whip cream, sugar and vanilla together until stiff. Frost top and sides.

Sprinkle top with chocolate shavings. Rich enough to serve 12.

Pictured on page 143.

RASPBERRY CHEESECAKE

With a marbled appearance, this is a mouth watering different type of baked cheesecake.

CRUST		
Butter or margarine	⅓ cup	75 mL
Graham cracker crumbs	1½ cups	375 mL
Brown sugar	¼ cup	50 mL

FILLING		
Cream cheese, softened	16 oz.	500 g
Granulated sugar	¾ cup	175 mL
Eggs	2	2
Lemon juice	1 tsp.	5 mL
Frozen raspberries, thawed and drained	15 oz.	425 g

TOPPING		
Sour cream	2 cups	500 mL
Granulated sugar	3 tbsp.	50 mL

Crust: Melt butter in medium size saucepan. Stir in crumbs and sugar. Pack into ungreased 10 inch (25 cm) springform or 9 x 9 inch (22 x 22 cm) pan. Bake in 350°F (180°C) oven for 10 minutes. Cool.

Filling: Beat cream cheese and sugar together well. Beat in eggs, 1 at a time, on low speed. Mix in lemon juice and raspberries. Turn into crumb-lined pan. Bake in 350°F (180°C) oven for about 35 to 45 minutes until firm. Let stand while preparing topping.

Topping: Mix sour cream and sugar together. Spread over cheesecake. Return to oven for 8 to 10 minutes. Chill until needed. Serve with Raspberry Sauce, page 135. Cuts into 12 pieces.

Pictured on page 125.

Pare Pointer

Have you heard about the blind carpenter? He picked up his hammer and saw.

So refreshing. Absolutely luscious. A favorite refrigerator dessert.

FIRST LAYER

All-purpose flour	2 cups	500 mL
Butter or margarine	1 cup	250 mL
Finely chopped pecans	1 cup	250 mL

SECOND LAYER

Cream cheese, softened	2 x 8 oz.	2 x 250 g
Icing (confectioner's) sugar	1 cup	250 mL
Whipping cream (or 1 env. topping)	1 cup	250 mL

THIRD LAYER

Lemon pudding and pie fillings (each makes 1 pie)	2	2

FOURTH LAYER

Whipping cream (or 2 env. topping)	2 cups	500 mL
Granulated sugar	2 tbsp.	30 mL
Vanilla	1 tsp.	5 mL

First Layer: Mix flour, butter and nuts together until crumbly. Press into 9 x 13 inch (22 x 33 cm) pan. Bake in 350°F (180°C) oven for 15 minutes. Cool.

Second Layer: Beat cheese and icing sugar together well. Beat whipping cream until stiff. Fold into cream cheese mixture. Spread over cooled crust.

Third Layer: Prepare lemon pie fillings according to directions on package. Cook, stirring often. Pour over cheese layer.

Fourth Layer: Beat cream, sugar and vanilla until stiff. Spread over lemon layer. Garnish with chopped pecans or slivered almonds. Makes 15 generous pieces.

Paré Pointer

Use yeast and polish and you will rise and shine.

QUICK PUDDING

Pudding and a yummy sauce cooked in the same dish.

All-purpose flour	1 cup	250 mL
Granulated sugar	½ cup	125 mL
Baking powder	2 tsp.	10 mL
Salt	⅛ tsp.	0.5 mL
Milk	½ cup	125 mL
Butter or margarine, softened	2 tbsp.	30 mL
Raisins	½ cup	125 mL
Cinnamon	½ tsp.	3 mL
Brown sugar, packed	1 cup	250 mL
Butter or margarine	1 tbsp.	15 mL
Vanilla	1 tsp.	5 mL
Hot water	2 cups	500 mL

Measure first 7 ingredients into bowl. Mix together with spoon. Turn into greased 8 inch (20 cm) casserole or pan.

In same bowl stir cinnamon, sugar, butter, vanilla and hot water until sugar dissolves. Pour over batter. Do not stir. Bake in 350°F (180°C) oven for about 30 minutes until sauce is on the bottom and top crust is firm to touch. Serves 6.

1. Chocolate Cherries page 134
2. Hazelnut Torte page 139
3. Peach Fluff page 132
4. Chocolate Strawberry Shortcake page 136

This light roll is always popular. Whether you choose jam, lemon filling or even pie filling, it will disappear in a hurry.

Eggs, room temperature	4	4
Granulated sugar	1 cup	250 mL
Water	¼ cup	60 mL
Vanilla	1 tsp.	5 mL
All-purpose flour	1 cup	250 mL
Baking powder	2 tsp.	10 mL
Salt	¼ tsp.	1 mL
Icing (confectioner's) sugar		

Grease 10 x 15 inch (25 x 38 cm) jelly roll pan. Line with waxed paper.

Beat eggs in mixing bowl until frothy. Add sugar and beat until light colored and thick.

Mix in water and vanilla.

Sift flour, baking powder and salt over egg mixture and fold in.

Turn into prepared pan. Bake in 400°F (200°C) oven for 12 to 15 minutes until an inserted toothpick comes out clean. Sift icing (confectioner's) sugar over tea towel. Turn cake out onto sugar. Peel off waxed paper. Trim crisp edges if any. Roll from narrow end, towel and cake together. Cool. Unroll. Fill with filling. Reroll.

RASPBERRY FILLING: Working quickly, raspberry jam can be spread over cake as soon as paper is peeled off. Roll cake, cover with towel and cool. Saves rerolling. Cuts into 10 to 15 pieces.

LEMON FILLING

Water	2 cups	500 mL
Cornstarch	6 tbsp.	100 mL
Granulated sugar	1½ cups	375 mL
Salt	¼ tsp.	1 mL
Lemon juice	½ cup	125 mL
Eggs	2	2

Heat water in saucepan over medium heat until boiling.

Stir cornstarch, sugar and salt together in bowl. Add lemon juice and eggs. Mix well. Pour, stirring, into boiling water. Cook and stir until it thickens. Cool, then spread over cake and roll.

PUMPKIN DESSERT

With soft pumpkin on the bottom and a thick crunchy top, this serves as many as two pumpkin pies.

Eggs	4	4
Granulated sugar	1 cup	250 mL
Canned pumpkin	28 oz.	796 mL
Cinnamon	1 tsp.	5 mL
Nutmeg	1 tsp.	5 mL
Ginger	1 tsp.	5 mL
Salt	1 tsp.	5 mL
Milk	3 cups	700 mL
Cake mix, yellow or white, 2 layer size	1	1
Butter or margarine	½ cup	125 mL
Finely chopped walnuts	⅓ cup	75 mL
Whipped cream or ice cream		

Beat eggs in large mixing bowl. Mix in next 7 ingredients in order given. Pour into greased 9 x 13 inch (22 x 33 cm) pan.

Put cake mix into bowl. Add butter and cut in until crumbly.

Mix in nuts. Sprinkle over pumpkin filling. Bake in 350°F (180°C) oven for about 1¼ to 1½ hours or until it tests done with toothpick.

Serve cold with whipped cream or hot with ice cream. Cuts into 12 generous or 15 average pieces.

STRAWBERRY SHORTCAKE

A summer classic that is good any time of year.

White layer cake, your own or a mix	1	1
Fresh strawberries	2 pts.	1 L
Granulated sugar to taste	2 - 3 tbsp.	30 - 50 mL
Whipping cream (or 1 env. topping)	1 cup	250 mL
Granulated sugar	1 tbsp.	15 mL
Vanilla	½ tsp.	2 mL

(continued on next page)

Place one layer of cake, flat side up, on serving plate.

Mash strawberries, adding sugar to taste. Spread ½ of the berries over cake layer. Place second layer, flat side down, over top. Spread second ½ of berries over the top layer. Cover and refrigerate until ready to serve.

Put cream, sugar and vanilla into bowl. Beat until stiff. Spread over the top layer of strawberries. Cut into wedges to serve. Serves 12.

RASPBERRY SHORTCAKE: Use fresh raspberries instead of straw-berries.

PEACH SHORTCAKE: Use fresh peaches, mashed or sliced, instead of strawberries.

CHOCOLATE SOUFFLÉ

Soft, moist and smooth. A delectable dessert. Serve with your favorite chocolate sauce or whipped cream.

Butter or margarine	2 tbsp.	30 mL
All-purpose flour	2 tbsp.	30 mL
Milk	¾ cup	175 mL
Unsweetened chocolate squares, cut up	2 x 1 oz.	2 x 28 g
Granulated sugar	⅓ cup	75 mL
Egg yolks, beaten	3	3
Egg whites	3	3
Vanilla	½ tsp.	2 mL

Melt butter in saucepan. Mix in flour. Add milk. Heat and stir until it boils and thickens.

Add chocolate and sugar. Stir until chocolate melts.

Add chocolate mixture slowly to beaten egg yolks, stirring well. Cool slightly.

Beat egg whites until stiff. Add vanilla. Fold into slightly cooled mixture. Spoon into greased 8 inch (20 cm) casserole, 3 inches (7.5 cm) deep. Set dish in pan of hot water. Bake in 350°F (180°C) oven for about 50 to 60 minutes until top is firm. Serves 4 to 6.

CRÈME CARAMEL

Usually associated with top-notch restaurants, this delicious custard, sauced in caramel, is much easier to make than you think. Only the explanation is lengthy.

Granulated sugar	**1 cup**	**250 mL**
Water	**½ cup**	**125 mL**
CUSTARD		
Eggs	**3**	**3**
Milk	**2 cups**	**500 mL**
Granulated sugar	**¼ cup**	**50 mL**
Salt	**¼ tsp.**	**1 mL**
Vanilla	**1 tsp.**	**5 mL**

Heat first amount of sugar in heavy pan over medium heat. Stir as sugar melts until completely melted and it turns a rich caramel color. If too light, it has no flavor, if too dark it will be bitter. Add water carefully. It will sputter with a vengeance. Stir until blended well. It will thicken as it blends. Pour into bottom of 6 custard cups, ring pan or casserole. Tilt cups (or container) to distribute caramelized sugar over bottom and part way up sides to coat well.

Custard: Beat eggs lightly in mixing bowl. Add milk, sugar, salt and vanilla. Beat together slightly. Pour into custard cups. Set cups in pan with ½ inch (1.5 cm) hot water in it. Bake in 325°F (160°C) oven for about 35 minutes until a knife inserted near outside edge comes out clean. Allow to cool ½ hour at room temperature. Chill for at least 3 hours. To unmold, run knife around edge. Dip bottom in hot water for a few moments. Place small plate over top and invert together. Remove cup. Serve to 6 lucky people.

CUSTARD: Omit first step of burning sugar and adding water. Mix custard, pour into 6½ inch (16 cm) casserole. Sprinkle with nutmeg. Place in pan of water. Bake in 325°F (160°C) oven for about 1 hour until a knife, inserted halfway between center and edge, comes out clean. Serve cold. Serves 4 to 6.

CUSTARD SAUCE: Pour beaten custard ingredients into top of double boiler. Omit nutmeg. Cook and stir over gently boiling water until mixture coats a metal spoon. Serve over fruit, pie, cake or ice cream.

CHOCOLATE CUSTARD: Add 2 tbsp. (30 mL) cocoa to Custard Sauce. Double amount of sugar.

BEST CHOCOLATE CHEESECAKE

So rich, so smooth — the ultimate. Freezes well.

CRUST

Butter or margarine	⅓ cup	75 mL
Graham cracker crumbs	1½ cups	350 mL
Granulated sugar	¼ cup	50 mL
Cocoa	¼ cup	50 mL

FILLING

Cream cheese, softened	3 x 8 oz.	3 x 250 g
Granulated sugar	1 cup	250 mL
Eggs	4	4
Sour cream	1 cup	250 mL
Semisweet chocolate chips	2 cups	450 mL
Butter or margarine	½ cup	125 mL

Crust: Melt butter in saucepan. Stir in crumbs, sugar and cocoa. Mix well. Press into bottom and ¾ way up sides of ungreased 10 inch (25 cm) springform pan. Do not bake.

Filling: Beat cream cheese and sugar until blended. Add eggs, 1 at a time, beating after each addition. Mix in sour cream.

Combine chocolate chips and butter in saucepan over low heat until melted. Stir often. Add to cheese mixture. Pour into prepared pan. Bake in 325°F (160°C) oven for about 1½ hours until center is firm. Cool at room temperature, then chill. To serve, top with whipped cream and shaved chocolate.

Variation: Fold in ½ cup (125 mL) chopped pecans or walnuts before baking.

Variation: Use whipping cream in place of sour cream for a milkier chocolate flavor.

Paré Pointer

Pity the minister named Mr. Fiddle. Now he is known as Fiddle D. D.

FROZEN LEMON MERINGUE

A frozen creation ready for company anytime. Lemon at its best.

CRUST

Butter or margarine	½ cup	125 mL
Graham cracker crumbs	2 cups	500 mL
Brown sugar, packed	⅓ cup	75 mL

FILLING

Egg yolks	6	6
Sweetened condensed milk	2 x 11 oz.	2 x 300 mL
Frozen lemonade, thawed	12 oz.	341 mL
Lemon juice	2 tbsp.	30 mL
Whipping cream (or 2 env. topping)	2 cups	500 mL

TOPPING

Egg whites, room temperature	6	6
Granulated sugar	¾ cup	175 mL

Crust: Melt butter in saucepan. Stir in crumbs and sugar. Press into ungreased 9 x 13 inch (22 x 33 cm) pan. Bake in 350° F (180° C) oven for 10 minutes.

Filling: Beat egg yolks until frothy. Beat in condensed milk, condensed lemonade and lemon juice. Beat until thick.

Beat cream until stiff. Fold into milk mixture. Spread over crust.

Topping: Beat egg whites until foamy. Add sugar gradually, beating until stiff. Spread over filling. Place under broiler for only a few seconds. Watch carefully. When golden, remove and cool. Freeze covered. To serve, remove from freezer for 15 to 20 minutes. Serve partially frozen. Serves 15 to 18.

Paré Pointer

Locomotion is a good description of a crazy dance.

An Italian favorite that made Sardi's famous. Meringue layers with chocolate, strawberries and cream.

MERINGUE

Egg whites, room temperature	6	6
Cream of tartar	¼ tsp.	1 mL
Granulated sugar	1½ cups	350 mL

FILLING

Semisweet chocolate chips	1 cup	250 mL
Water	3 tbsp.	50 mL
Whipping cream	3 cups	750 mL
Granulated sugar	5 tbsp.	75 mL
Vanilla	2 tsp.	10 mL
Fresh strawberries, sliced lengthwise — save a few for garnish	3 cups	750 mL

Meringue: Beat egg whites and cream of tartar until soft peaks form. Beat in sugar gradually, beating until stiff and glossy. Line 3 round 8 inch (20 cm) pans with foil or outline 3 circles, 8 inch (20 cm), on foil-lined cookie sheets. Very lightly grease the foil. Divide and spread the meringue evenly among the pans. Bake in 250°F (130°C) oven for about 45 minutes until dry and crispy firm. Cool on racks. Peel off foil.

Filling: In heavy saucepan, melt chips with water over low heat. Spread over 2 meringue shells.

Whip cream, sugar and vanilla until stiff. Spread over all 3 meringue layers. Place 1 layer with chocolate on serving plate. Spoon ½ strawberries over top. Place second layer with chocolate over first on plate. Spoon second ½ strawberries over top. Add third layer. Garnish with whole berries. Chill 2 or 3 hours before serving. Serves 8.

STRAWBERRY MERINGUE SHORTCAKE: Beat first 3 ingredients only. Shape into several smaller meringues with raised sides. To serve, fill with sweetened strawberries and top with whipped cream.

LETTUCE EGG TOSS

A superb additional way to serve lettuce. If eggs are in good supply, add another one or two.

Lettuce, solid medium head	½	½
Green onions, sliced (optional)	3 - 5	3 - 5
Hard boiled eggs, cut up	2	2
Salad dressing to coat		

Tear or cut lettuce into bite size pieces. Add onions and eggs. Add salad dressing. Toss and serve. Serves 6 to 8.

EGG MUSHROOM TOSS: Add ½ to 1 cup (125 to 250 mL) sliced fresh mushrooms before tossing.

LETTUCE CHEESE SALAD: Eggs may be omitted if preferred. Add ½ to 1 cup (125 to 250 mL) grated or diced medium Cheddar cheese. Colorful, healthy, good!

Pictured on page 215.

CREAMY CUCUMBER MOLD

A wonderful way to serve cucumbers and sour cream. This tastes every bit as good as it looks.

Lime flavored gelatin	3 oz.	85 g
Boiling water	1 cup	225 mL
Salt	½ tsp.	2 mL
Onion powder	¼ tsp.	1 mL
Lemon juice	1 tsp.	5 mL
Sour cream	1 cup	250 mL
Mayonnaise	⅓ cup	75 mL
Cucumber, peeled, seeded, chopped and drained	1	1

Dissolve gelatin in boiling water. Stir in salt, onion powder and lemon juice. Chill until syrupy. Stir occasionally.

Add sour cream and mayonnaise. Fold in until blended.

Fold in cucumber. Transfer to 3 cup (700 mL) mold. Chill. Serves 8.

ORANGE ALMOND SALAD

Pretty, nutty and delicious. Tops for a first course.

Romaine lettuce	1	1
Orange segments, drained	10 oz.	284 mL
Green onions, sliced	2	2
Slivered almonds, toasted	¼ cup	50 mL
Salad oil	¼ cup	50 mL
Vinegar	¼ cup	50 mL
Granulated sugar	¼ cup	50 mL

Tear lettuce into bite size pieces. Arrange over salad plates. Place equal number of orange segments on each bed of lettuce. Scatter green onions over top. Sprinkle with almonds.

Stir salad oil, vinegar and sugar together well. Pour over salad. Serve. Makes 4 to 6 servings.

Note: Toast almonds in pan in 350°F (180°C) oven for about 5 minutes until golden.

Pictured on back cover.

OIL AND VINEGAR DRESSING

Such a simple recipe and also one of the most requested. It is better to add oil and vinegar separately to avoid the oil (which stays at the top) all coming out with the very first pouring. Very economical. A life saver for lettuce.

Vinegar	3 cups	750 mL
Granulated sugar	4 cups	1 L

Salad oil as needed to serve

Combine vinegar and sugar in container. Stir, stir and stir! It will eventually dissolve. Store in cool place. Will keep for months. To use, pour equal amounts of oil and vinegar-sugar dressing over salad and toss. Oil may be cut down if desired. You will know when you have enough dressing. Too much and it will sink to the bottom of the bowl. Don't sprinkle salt over salad as it takes away the tartness of the dressing.

LEMON CHEDDAR SALAD

This must be the quickest of the special salads. Showy and extremely good. A party special.

Lemon flavored gelatin	3 oz.	85 g
Boiling water	1 cup	225 mL
Crushed pineapple and juice	14 oz.	398 mL
Whipping cream (or 1 env. topping)	1 cup	250 mL
Grated Cheddar cheese	1 cup	250 mL

Combine gelatin and boiling water in bowl. Stir to dissolve.

Stir in crushed pineapple and juice. Chill until of egg white consistency.

Whip cream until stiff. Fold into thickened jelly. Fold in grated cheese. Pour into your prettiest bowl. Chill. Garnish with orange slices if desired. Serves 10.

MARSHMALLOW CHEDDAR: Add 1 cup (250 mL) small marshmallows with whipped cream and grated cheese.

FESTIVE EGGNOG SALAD

But it has no eggnog in it! Festive is the word and it does taste like eggnog. A beautiful red base topped with a yellow crown.

Vanilla pudding mix (not instant), 4 portion size	1	1
Lemon flavored gelatin	3 oz.	85 g
Water	2 cups	450 mL
Lemon juice	2 tbsp.	30 mL
Raspberry flavored gelatin	3 oz.	85 g
Boiling water	1 cup	225 mL
Whole cranberry sauce	2 cups	450 mL
Celery, finely chopped	½ cup	125 mL
Pecans or walnuts, finely chopped	⅓ cup	75 mL
Whipping cream (or 1 env. topping)	1 cup	250 mL
Nutmeg	½ tsp.	2 mL

(continued on next page)

Put pudding mix and lemon gelatin into medium size saucepan. Gradually stir in water and lemon juice. Cook and stir over medium heat until boiling. Remove from heat. Chill until syrupy.

In medium size bowl combine raspberry gelatin with boiling water. Stir to dissolve. Mix in cranberry sauce, celery and nuts. Chill until thickening stage.

Whip cream until stiff and fold into thickened pudding and jelly mixture. Fold in nutmeg. Pour into mold. Chill until a bit firm then pour thickened cranberry mixture over top. Chill overnight. Unmolded on frilly looking lettuce, this highlights any table. Serves 10 to 12.

SPINACH SALAD

The dressing makes this different from the usual.

DRESSING

Commercial salad dressing	½ cup	125 mL
Commercial coleslaw dressing	¼ cup	50 mL
Dried dill weed	¼ tsp.	1 mL

Combine all together. Stir. Set aside.

SALAD

Large bunch of spinach leaves	1	1
Swiss cheese, shredded	¼ cup	50 mL
Cheddar cheese, shredded	¼ cup	50 mL
Sliced mushrooms	1 cup	250 mL
Bacon slices, cooked and crumbled	6	6
Hard boiled eggs, chopped	2	2

Tear clean spinach leaves into large bowl. Add about ¾ dressing. Toss to coat. Pile onto four to six salad plates.

Sprinkle shredded cheese over top followed by mushrooms, crumbled bacon and chopped egg. Drizzle a bit of dressing over top. Serve immediately. Serves 4 to 6.

Variation: Omit Swiss and increase Cheddar to ½ cup (125 mL), shredded for equally good results.

ROMAINE SALAD: Substitute Romaine lettuce for the spinach leaves. Delicious and easier to obtain at times than spinach.

LAYERED TURKEY SALAD

An impressive looking salad that you make a day ahead. Some dinner buns and a rich dessert complete a great meal.

Shredded head lettuce	6 cups	1.5 L
Medium cucumber, scored, thinly sliced	1	1
Bean sprouts	1 cup	250 mL
Green onions, chopped	6	6
Cooked turkey, cut in matchstick size pieces	4 cups	1 L
Frozen pea pods, thawed (or use cooked peas)	12 oz.	341 mL
Mayonnaise	2 cups	500 mL
Granulated sugar	1 tbsp.	15 mL
Curry powder	2 tsp.	10 mL
Ginger powder	½ tsp.	2 mL

Layer first 6 ingredients in order given in a glass bowl so the layers will show.

Mix mayonnaise, sugar, curry powder and ginger together. Spoon dabs here and there over top. Spread to cover to edge of bowl. Cover. Chill overnight. Serves 8.

Pictured on page 89.

GREEN GODDESS SALAD

Just a great addition to any meal.

Head lettuce, medium	2	2
Mayonnaise	1 cup	250 mL
Sour cream	½ cup	125 mL
Chopped green onion	¼ cup	50 mL
Chopped parsley	¼ cup	50 mL
Anchovy paste	2 tsp.	10 mL
Worcestershire sauce	1 tsp.	5 mL
Prepared mustard	½ tsp.	2 mL
Salt	½ tsp.	2 mL
Pepper	⅛ tsp.	0.5 mL
Garlic powder (or 1 clove, minced)	¼ tsp.	1 mL
Cooked crab or shrimp	1 cup	250 mL

(continued on next page)

Have lettuce in bite size pieces in refrigerator.

Combine remaining ingredients except seafood in bowl. Beat with spoon to blend. Makes 2 cups (500 mL) dressing.

To serve, put lettuce, dressing and crab into large bowl. Toss well. Serves 12 to 15.

Pictured on page 161.

CREAMY LETTUCE SALAD

Little chunks of cucumber with celery seed look nice throughout. Tasty.

DRESSING

Sour cream	½ cup	125 mL
Mayonnaise	½ cup	125 mL
Onion powder	¼ tsp.	1 mL
Celery seed	¼ tsp.	1 mL
Salt	¼ tsp.	1 mL
Dash of cayenne pepper		
Finely diced, peeled cucumber	½ cup	125 mL

SALAD

Head lettuce or salad greens	1	1
Sliced green onions	3	3
Radish, thinly sliced	6	6
Green pepper strips	¼ cup	50 mL

Dressing: Mix all ingredients together. Chill until needed. Makes 1 cup (250 mL).

Salad: Combine lettuce or greens, onion, radish and green pepper in large bowl. Add about ½ dressing and toss. Add more dressing to taste. Serves 8.

Paré Pointer

It would be a lot easier to recognize everyone's horses if they would quit switching their tails.

CREAMY CAESAR

This has a thick creamy dressing. Excellent salad.

DRESSING

Garlic clove	1	1
Large egg (or 2 smaller)	1	1
Worcestershire sauce	1 tsp.	5 mL
Lemon juice	2 tbsp.	30 mL
Anchovy paste	2 tsp.	10 mL
Dash of pepper		
Salad oil	1 cup	250 mL

Put first six ingredients into blender. Blend until smooth.

Add oil in fine stream while blending to thicken. Chill about 2 hours.

SALAD

Large head Romaine lettuce	1	1
Croutons	2 cups	500 mL
Bacon slices, cooked and crumbled	8	8
Parmesan cheese	½ cup	125 mL

Tear lettuce in bite size pieces in salad bowl. Add croutons. Add dressing. Toss to coat.

Sprinkle with bacon and cheese.

CROUTONS

Butter or margarine	2 tbsp.	30 mL
Garlic clove, sliced	1	1
White bread slices, cubed	4 - 5	4 - 5

Sauté garlic in butter for 2 to 3 minutes. Remove garlic and discard. Add bread cubes. Fry until golden, stirring often. Remove. Cool.

Paré Pointer

Adam and Eve could have gambled a lot if they chose. After all, they had a par-a-dise.

JAPANESE CHICKEN SALAD

Fantastic for lunch accompanied with hot, crusty rolls. Make it the night before and be ready for compliments.

SALAD

Sesame seeds, toasted	2 tbsp.	30 mL
Slivered almonds, toasted	½ cup	125 mL
Cooked chicken, cubed	2 cups	500 mL
Small head of cabbage, shredded	1	1
Instant chicken noodles, crumbled (See Note)	3 oz.	85 g
Chopped green onions	2	2

DRESSING

Package of noodle seasoning	1	1
Salad oil	½ cup	125 mL
Vinegar	3 tbsp.	50 mL
Granulated sugar	1 tbsp.	15 mL
Monosodium glutamate	1 tsp.	5 mL
Salt	1 tsp.	5 mL
Pepper	½ tsp.	2 mL

Salad: Put sesame seeds and almonds in single layer in pan. Toast in 350° F (180° C) oven for 5 minutes or so until golden. Watch carefully after 5 minutes so they don't get too brown. Remove from oven. Set aside.

Put chicken into large bowl. Add cabbage, crumbled noodles and onions.

Dressing: In small bowl combine packet of seasoning, oil, vinegar, sugar, monosodium glutamate, salt and pepper. Stir together. Pour over chicken-cabbage mixture. Stir. Store in covered bowl overnight in refrigerator to marinate. Just before serving sprinkle with sesame seeds and slivered almonds. Toss lightly to distribute. Serves 6.

Note: The instant chicken noodles come in 3 oz. (85 g) packages. They can be found in the soup section of grocery stores. There are Japanese, Chinese and other brands.

MEXICAN SALAD

A main meal salad. Add crusty brown dinner rolls and dig in.

TACO SHELLS		
Flour tortillas	**6 - 8**	**6 - 8**
Fat for deep-frying		
SALAD		
Head lettuce, cut up	**1**	**1**
Grated medium Cheddar cheese	**2 cups**	**500 mL**
Kidney beans, rinsed and drained	**14 oz.**	**398 mL**
Small onion, diced or sliced	**1**	**1**
Tomatoes, diced or sliced	**2**	**2**
Catalina dressing (or Russian)	**¾ cup**	**175 mL**
Corn chips, broken up, for garnish (optional)	**⅔ cup**	**150 mL**

Taco Shells: Using soup ladle or empty can, push on center of tortilla down into hot 375° F (190° C) fat. It will be necessary to use an oven mitt for protection from the extreme heat unless ladle has a long handle. Keep tortilla completely immersed until lightly browned, bubbled and bowl shaped. Drain upside down on paper towel-lined tray. These can be prepared ahead.

Salad: Put first 6 ingredients into bowl. Toss to coat. Spoon into taco shells.

Sprinkle chips over top. Makes 6 to 8 servings.

Pictured on page 161.

1. Whole Tomato Aspic page 163
2. Rich Tea Biscuits page 40
3. Mexican Salad page 160
4. Tuna Salad page 170
5. Green Goddess Salad page 156

WHOLE TOMATO ASPIC

This aspic uses canned tomatoes. Don't let the raspberry gelatin throw you. It is a tasty combination.

Raspberry flavored gelatin	3 oz.	85 g
Canned tomatoes, mashed	19 oz.	540 mL
Vinegar	1 tbsp.	15 mL
Basil	½ tsp.	2 mL
Onion powder (optional)	⅛ tsp.	0.5 mL
Salt, small sprinkle		
Pepper, smaller sprinkle		
Chopped celery	½ cup	125 mL

Combine first 7 ingredients together in saucepan. Heat and stir over low heat to dissolve gelatin powder. Remove from heat. Chill until syrupy.

Add celery. Stir. Pour into 4 cup (1 L) mold. Chill. May be garnished with mayonnaise and a whole raspberry if desired. Serves 8.

Pictured on page 161.

CRANBERRY BANANA SALAD

For a special lunch or snack, serve this on a lettuce leaf, with baking powder biscuits or rolls.

Lemon flavored gelatin powder	3 oz.	85 g
Boiling water	1¼ cups	300 mL
Whole cranberry sauce	14 oz.	398 mL
Medium bananas, sliced	2	2
Finely chopped nuts	⅓ cup	75 mL
Mayonnaise for garnish		
Nuts for garnish		

Dissolve gelatin in boiling water. Stir in cranberry sauce. Chill until syrupy.

Fold bananas and nuts into thickened jelly. Pour into 4 cup (900 mL) mold or serving bowl. Chill. Garnish with small dollops of mayonnaise sprinkled with nuts. Also may be chilled in an 8 x 8 inch (20 x 20 cm) pan for serving in squares on a bed of lettuce. Cuts into 9 squares.

MULTI-LAYERED SALAD

There is only one word to describe this salad — amazing! Amazing how fresh it stays when made the day before. Read footnotes before making.

Medium head of lettuce with some spinach or Romaine mixed in	1	1
Sliced celery	1 cup	250 mL
Hard boiled eggs, chopped or sliced	6	6
Cooked peas, fresh or frozen	10 oz.	284 g
Chopped green pepper	½ cup	125 mL
Green onions, sliced	8	8
Water chestnuts, sliced thinly	6 oz.	170 mL
Bacon slices, cooked and crumbled	8	8
Mayonnaise	1 cup	250 mL
Sour cream	1 cup	250 mL
Granulated sugar	2 tbsp.	30 mL
Cheddar cheese, grated	1 cup	250 mL
Bacon slices, cooked and crumbled	4	4

Cut or break lettuce into small pieces. Layer in bottom of 9 x 13 inch (22 x 33 cm) pan. Scatter each layer in order given.

Mix mayonnaise with sour cream and sugar. Spread over top being careful to seal right to the edge of pan.

Scatter grated cheese over followed by bacon. Seal well with plastic wrap. Store in refrigerator for at least 24 hours before serving. Cut into squares. Serves 10 to 12.

Notes: Depending on your likes, dislikes and possible allergies, several layers can be omitted. The most common layers are lettuce, eggs, peas, onions, bacon and mayonnaise.

LETTUCE: A mixture of greens is a good base.

PEAS: May be layered uncooked. Many do prefer raw.

BACON: May be used as a layer, as a top garnish or as both. Less bacon is needed when used only as a topping.

MAYONNAISE: Salad dressing may be used instead.

SOUR CREAM: Double the mayonnaise and omit sour cream if preferred.

(continued on next page)

CHEDDAR CHEESE: A lesser amount may be used for top garnish. Swiss cheese may be substituted. Also a heavy layer of Romano or Parmesan cheese may be substituted.

GARNISH: To have greens on top, sprinkle a few slices of green onion over all.

CONTAINER: A glass bowl shows off this salad. It makes the task of getting some of each layer a bit difficult.

FOO YONG SUPREME

A Foo Yong Salad to end all Foo Yong Salads. Definitely the pick of them all. Prepare salad ahead but toss at the last moment.

DRESSING

Salad oil	¼ cup	50 mL
Granulated sugar	¼ cup	50 mL
Vinegar	2 tbsp.	30 mL
Ketchup	2⅔ tbsp.	40 mL
Grated onion	1 tbsp.	15 mL
Worcestershire sauce	1 tsp.	5 mL

Mix all ingredients together. Store in small covered bowl overnight if time permits.

SALAD

Large head Romaine lettuce	1	1
Bacon strips, cooked and crumbled	5	5
Generous handful bean sprouts (fresh is best)	1	1
Hard boiled eggs, chopped finely	2	2

Tear lettuce into bite size pieces. Sprinkle cold, crumbled bacon over top, then bean sprouts followed by chopped eggs. Can be prepared to this point, then refrigerated until the last minute. Pour all of the dressing over top. Toss together and serve at once. Serves 6.

Note: Head lettuce can be used instead of Romaine if you are preparing for a crowd. A large quantity can be cut up in no time. Add a portion of Romaine lettuce for looks.

COLESLAW FOREVER

With this in the refrigerator you will never be caught short without a salad. Keeps and keeps and keeps.

Large cabbage, shredded	1	1
Medium carrots, grated	2	2
Medium onion, grated	1	1
Vinegar	¾ cup	175 mL
Salad oil	½ cup	125 mL
Granulated sugar	1½ cups	325 mL
Salt	1 tbsp.	15 mL
Celery seed	1 tbsp.	15 mL

Put cabbage, carrots and onion into large bowl.

Measure vinegar, oil, sugar, salt and celery seed into large saucepan. Bring to boil, stirring frequently. Pour hot over cabbage mixture. Stir to mix, pressing down until vegetables wilt and are covered with brine. Cool. Store in covered container in refrigerator. Let stand one or two days before eating. Keeps for weeks and weeks. Darkens a bit with age.

BEAN SPROUT SALAD

A touch of the orient. Delicious.

Bean sprouts	12 oz.	350 g
Green onions, sliced	¼ cup	50 mL
Salad oil (peanut or sesame is best)	2 tbsp.	30 mL
Soy sauce	2 tbsp.	30 mL
Sesame seeds toasted	2 tbsp.	30 mL
Granulated sugar	1 tbsp.	15 mL
Vinegar	1 tbsp.	15 mL
Pimiento or red pepper strips	¼ cup	50 mL

Put bean sprouts and onions into bowl.

In small bowl combine salad oil, soy sauce, sesame seeds, sugar, vinegar and pimiento. Stir to mix. Pour over sprouts and onions. Toss to coat. Serves 4 to 6.

Note: Toast sesame seeds in 350° F (180° C) oven for about 5 minutes until golden.

PINEAPPLE CREAM SALAD

Rich and creamy — everybody's favorite. My favorite.

Lemon flavored gelatin	3 oz.	85 g
Boiling water	1 cup	225 mL
Crushed pineapple and juice	14 oz.	398 mL
Cream cheese	4 oz.	125 g
Small marshmallows	100	100
Whipping cream (or 1 env. topping)	1 cup	250 mL

Combine gelatin with boiling water in fairly large bowl. Stir to dissolve.

Add pineapple with juice. Using wire cheese cutter, cut in cheese. Add marshmallows. Stir. Chill until it begins to thicken, stirring occasionally.

Whip cream until stiff. Fold into thickened mixture. Pour into a pretty serving bowl. Chill. This salad doesn't hold very well since it isn't too firm but will stand for a short time if molded. Serves 12.

SEVEN UP SALAD

A cool lime colored melt-in-your-mouth goodness.

Seven Up soft drink (or other)	1 cup	250 mL
Small marshmallows	2 cups	500 mL
Lime flavored gelatin	3 oz.	85 g
Cream cheese, cut up	8 oz.	250 g
Crushed pineapple with juice	14 oz.	398 mL
Whipping cream (or 1 env. topping)	1 cup	250 mL
Salad dressing	½ cup	125 mL

Put Seven Up and marshmallows into medium saucepan. Heat and stir over medium heat to melt marshmallows.

Stir in gelatin to dissolve. Add cream cheese. Stir until melted. Remove from heat. Stir in pineapple. Chill until syrupy.

Whip cream until stiff. Add salad dressing. Fold into thickened jelly. Pour into mold or pretty serving bowl. Chill. Serves 10 to 12.

TWENTY FOUR HOUR SALAD

A delicious salad, fruity and creamy. A good make ahead.

Eggs	2	2
Granulated sugar	2 tbsp.	30 mL
Vinegar	2 tbsp.	30 mL
Pineapple juice	2 tbsp.	30 mL
Butter or margarine	1 tbsp.	15 mL
Pinch of salt		
Fruit cocktail, drained	14 oz.	398 mL
Pineapple pieces, drained	14 oz.	398 mL
Seedless grapes, halved, optional	½ cup	125 mL
Banana, sliced	1	1
Small marshmallows	2 cups	500 mL
Whipping cream (or 1 env. topping)	1 cup	250 mL

Beat eggs with spoon in top of double boiler. Stir in sugar, vinegar, pineapple juice, butter and salt. Cook and stir over boiling water until thickened. Chill thoroughly.

Add well drained fruit cocktail and pineapple to egg mixture. Add grapes, banana and marshmallows.

Whip cream until stiff. Fold into fruit. Chill for twenty four hours or overnight.

PEACHES AND CREAM

Such a pretty salad. A shimmering delight.

Peach flavored gelatin	3 oz.	85 g
Boiling water	1 cup	225 mL
Peach juice (add water if needed)	1 cup	225 mL
Almond flavoring	¼ tsp.	1 mL
Whipping cream (or 1 env. topping)	1 cup	250 mL
Sliced peaches, drained	14 oz.	398 mL

(continued on next page)

Dissolve gelatin in boiling water in medium size bowl.

Add juice and flavoring. Stir. Measure out 1 cup (225 mL) jelly into medium size bowl and chill until syrupy. Leave remainder of jelly at room temperature.

Whip cream until stiff. Fold into the thickened jelly. Pour into mold. Chill. Put remainder of jelly in refrigerator to chill until syrupy.

Fold peaches into thickened clear jelly. Spoon over first layer. Chill until firm. Serves 6.

CHERRY CHEESE SALAD

Just right for a bridal shower, a ladies meeting or a club get-together. Serve with parkerhouse rolls. A creamy lemon top layer over a red base.

Raspberry flavored gelatin	3 oz.	85 g
Boiling water	1 cup	225 mL
Cherry pie filling	19 oz.	540 mL
Lemon flavored gelatin	3 oz.	85 g
Boiling water	1 cup	225 mL
Cream cheese	4 oz.	125 g
Mayonnaise	1/3 cup	75 mL
Crushed pineapple with juice	1 cup	225 mL
Whipping cream (or 1 env. topping)	1 cup	250 mL
Small white marshmallows	1½ cups	375 mL
Chopped nuts	2 tbsp.	30 mL
Lettuce		

Dissolve raspberry gelatin in boiling water. Stir in pie filling. Pour into 9 x 9 inch (22 x 22 cm) pan. Chill until almost set then pour on next layer.

Dissolve lemon gelatin in boiling water. Set aside.

Have cream cheese at room temperature. Beat cheese and mayonnaise together in small bowl. Mix in dissolved lemon gelatin. Stir in pineapple with juice. Chill until syrupy.

Whip cream until stiff. Fold into lemon gelatin. Add marshmallows and fold in. Pour over cherry layer. Sprinkle nuts over top. Chill.

Serve on shredded or leaf lettuce. Cuts into 9 or 12 thick portions.

TUNA SALAD

A perfect dress-up for tuna. Creamy good.

Lemon flavored gelatin	3 oz.	85 g
Boiling water	1 cup	250 mL
Condensed chicken rice soup	10 oz.	284 mL
Canned tuna, drained	7 oz.	198 g
Finely chopped celery	1 cup	250 mL
Peas, cooked and cooled	1 cup	250 mL
Chopped pecans or walnuts	½ cup	125 mL
Whipping cream (or 1 env. topping)	1 cup	250 mL
Mayonnaise	½ cup	125 mL

Stir gelatin powder into boiling water to dissolve. Add condensed soup. Mix. Chill until syrupy.

Add tuna, celery, peas and nuts.

Whip cream until stiff. Add mayonnaise. Mix. Fold into gelatin mixture. Spoon into serving bowl. Chill. Unmold and garnish with lemon slices and parsley. Serves 8 to 10.

Pictured on page 161.

AVOCADO MOLD

If you have never used avocado before, this is a good way to start. You will be won over.

Lime flavored gelatin	3 oz.	85 g
Boiling water	1 cup	225 mL
Mayonnaise	½ cup	125 mL
Cream cheese, cut in	4 oz.	125 g
Avocado, peeled and mashed	1	1
Chopped celery	¾ cup	175 mL
Chopped pimiento	1 tbsp.	15 mL
Dry onion flakes	1 tbsp.	15 mL
Garlic salt	⅛ tsp.	0.5 mL

Dissolve gelatin in boiling water.

Add remaining ingredients in order given. Mix well. Pour into 4 cup (1 L) mold. Chill. Stir occasionally while chilling. Chill several hours. Serves 8.

Creamy thick chowder with bright bits of carrot perking up the color. Can easily be doubled or halved. To freeze, omit white sauce and potato.

Finely diced celery	1 cup	250 mL
Finely diced carrot	1 cup	250 mL
Finely diced onion	1 cup	250 mL
Diced potato	1 cup	250 mL
Water	2 cups	500 mL
Milk	7 cups	1.75 L
Butter or margarine, melted	1 cup	250 mL
All-purpose flour	1 cup	250 mL
Salt	2 tsp.	10 mL
Pepper	1 tsp.	5 mL
Milk	1 cup	250 mL
Canned baby clams with juice	10 oz.	284 g
Parsley for garnish		

Put first 5 ingredients into large pot. Simmer, covered, until tender. Do not drain.

In large heavy saucepan, heat first amount of milk.

Stir butter, flour, salt and pepper together well in bowl. Whisk in second amount of milk until smooth. Pour into hot milk and stir until it boils and thickens. Add vegetables with liquid.

Stir in clams with juice. An additional 5 oz. (142 g) of clams with juice may be added if you wish. Heat through. Garnish with fresh chopped parsley. Makes about 12 cups (3 L).

Pare Pointer

Dogs have to be experts on trees so they don't bark up the wrong one.

CORN SOUP

This wonderful soup has been a family favorite forever.

Milk	3½ cups	800 mL
Finely chopped onion (optional)	2 tbsp.	30 mL
Butter or margarine	1 tsp.	5 mL
Canned cream style corn	28 oz.	796 mL
Milk	½ cup	125 mL
All-purpose flour	2 tbsp.	30 mL
Salt	1 tsp.	5 mL
Pepper	⅛ tsp.	0.5 mL
Butter, chives or parsley for garnish		

Heat first amount of milk in large heavy saucepan.

Sauté onion in butter until clear and soft. Put in cone ricer.

Add corn to onion. Press through cone ricer. If you don't have a cone ricer, onion and corn may be puréed in blender. Rub through strainer if it isn't smooth enough.

Mix second amount of milk with flour, salt and pepper until no lumps remain. Stir into hot milk until it boils and thickens. Add corn and onion mixture. Heat through. Serve with a dab of butter, chopped chives or parsley. Makes about 7½ cups (1.7 L).

CHICKEN SOUP

Cream corn adds flavor. A good combination.

Chicken stock	2 cups	500 mL
Canned cream style corn	14 oz.	398 mL
Finely chopped chicken	2 cups	500 mL
Dry onion flakes	2 tsps.	10 mL
Water	¼ cup	60 mL
All-purpose flour	2 tbsp.	30 mL
Salt	½ tsp.	2 mL
Pepper	⅛ tsp.	0.5 mL
Toasted sesame seeds for garnish		
Chopped ham for garnish		

(continued on next page)

Put chicken stock, corn, chicken and onion flakes into saucepan. Bring to a boil.

Mix water, flour, salt and pepper together until no lumps remain. Stir into boiling soup to thicken.

Garnish with sesame seeds and ham to serve. Makes 4½ cups (1.1 L).

BEEF BARLEY SOUP

A meaty soup guaranteed to please every appetite. Freeze portion size for a continuing supply. Extra good. Use leftover roast beef.

Water	6 cups	1.5 L
Beef bouillon cubes - ⅕ oz. (6 g) size	6	6
Canned tomatoes, mashed	28 oz.	796 mL
Condensed tomato soup	10 oz.	284 mL
Shredded carrot	2 cups	500 mL
Shredded potato	2 cups	500 mL
Chopped onion	1½ cups	375 mL
Chopped celery	1 cup	250 mL
Pearl or pot barley	½ cup	125 mL
Water	6 cups	1.5 L
Parsley flakes	1 tbsp.	15 mL
Granulated sugar	1 tsp.	5 mL
Salt	1 tsp.	5 mL
Pepper	¼ tsp.	1 mL
Thyme	¼ tsp.	1 mL
Cooked roast beef, chopped	3 cups	750 mL

Heat first amount of water and bouillon cubes in large pot. Stir to dissolve.

Add remaining ingredients except beef. Bring to boil. Cover and simmer slowly for about 1½ hours.

Add beef and simmer ½ hour more. Makes about 22 cups (5 L).

HAMBURGER SOUP: Omit chopped roast beef. Scramble fry 2 lbs. (1 kg) lean ground beef. Add to soup halfway through cooking. Part ground beef and part roast beef may be used also.

CORN CREAM CHEESE SOUP

The cream cheese enhances this soup to make it different from others. A good rich choice for a sit down appetizer.

Cream cheese, softened	8 oz.	250 g
Chicken bouillon cube - ⅕ oz. (6 g) size	1	1
Canned cream style corn	14 oz.	398 mL
Milk	1 cup	250 mL
Water	1 cup	250 mL
Finely chopped green pepper	¼ cup	50 mL
Finely chopped onion	¼ cup	50 mL
Salt	½ tsp.	2 mL
Pepper	⅛ tsp.	0.5 mL

Chopped fresh parsley for garnish

Cut cheese into chunks and put into blender. Add bouillon cube and corn. Blend until smooth. Set aside.

Put milk and water into saucepan. Add green pepper, onion, salt and pepper. Bring to boil. Cover and simmer until vegetables are tender. Add cheese mixture. Reheat, stirring often, until just below boiling point.

Serve garnished with parsley. Makes about 5 cups (1.25 L).

OYSTER SOUP

A good choice for the oyster set. The vegetables add texture to the broth.

Butter or margarine	¼ cup	50 mL
Chopped onion	¼ cup	50 mL
Chopped celery	¼ cup	50 mL
All-purpose flour	¼ cup	50 mL
Salt	1 tsp.	5 mL
Pepper	¼ tsp.	1 mL
Parsley flakes	2 tsp.	10 mL
Rich milk	4 cups	900 mL
Can of small oysters with juice	5 oz.	142 g

(continued on next page)

Combine butter, onion and celery in saucepan. Sauté until clear and soft. Do not brown.

Mix in flour, salt, pepper and parsley. Stir in milk until it boils and thickens.

Add oysters with juice. Heat. Makes a scant 5 cups (1 L).

Note: If using fresh or frozen oysters, simmer until their edges curl, about 5 minutes.

BEET SOUP

Tomatoes add to the rich flavor of this soup. For a full meal with outstanding taste try the Hamburger Borscht.

Stewed tomatoes	14 oz.	398 mL
Canned beets, diced or cut into strips, with juice	2 x 14 oz.	2 x 398 mL
Medium carrot, grated	1	1
Medium onion, chopped	1	1
Beef broth	4 cups	1 L
Medium potato, grated	1	1
Shredded cabbage, packed	3 cups	675 mL
Small green pepper, diced	1	1
Ketchup	1/3 cup	75 mL
Dill seeds	1/4 tsp.	1 mL
Salt	1/2 tsp.	2 mL
Pepper	1/4 tsp.	1 mL
Sour cream		

Combine first 12 ingredients together in large pot. Bring to boil. Cover and simmer about 30 minutes. If dill flavor is too faint using first amount, add more. Simmer to blend flavor.

Serve with a dab of sour cream or pass a bowl of sour cream separately. Makes about 11 cups (2.5 L).

HAMBURGER BORSCHT: Scramble fry 1 lb. (500 g) lean ground beef. Add to soup. Makes more of a meal yet. This could be one of your favorite soups.

TOMATO RICE SOUP

The secret ingredient is citric acid — not a necessity but worth buying at your local drugstore for this recipe alone.

Water	6 cups	1.5 L
Condensed tomato soup	20 oz.	598 mL
Canned tomato paste	5½ oz.	156 mL
Cooked rice	1½ cups	375 mL
Seasoned salt	1 tsp.	5 mL
Pepper	½ tsp.	2 mL
Parsley flakes	1 tsp.	5 mL
Citric acid	¼ tsp.	1 mL

Combine all ingredients in large saucepan. Simmer together for 5 minutes. Makes 4½ cups (1 L).

Variation: Use some milk in place of the water for a creamed look.

NEPTUNE CHOWDER

A cheese-flavored fish soup. Try it with or without any fishing luck. This is good without adding any cheese at all and is super if double the amount is added. Freezes well.

Butter or margarine	2 tbsp.	30 mL
Thinly sliced onion	2 cups	500 mL
Chopped celery	1 cup	250 mL
Diced potato	2 cups	500 mL
Sliced carrot	1 cup	250 mL
Water	2 cups	500 mL
Salt	1 tsp.	5 mL
Pepper	¼ tsp.	1 mL
Fish fillets, fresh or frozen, cut bite size	1 lb.	454 g
Milk	2 cups	500 mL
Mild process cheese	4 oz.	125 g
(Velveeta is good)		
Chives or parsley for garnish		

(continued on next page)

Put butter, onion and celery into large saucepan. Sauté until onion is clear and soft.

Add potato, carrot, water, salt and pepper. Bring to boil. Cover and simmer about 10 minutes.

Add fish and simmer 10 minutes more.

Add milk and cheese. Heat, stirring often, until cheese melts. Do not boil. Season to taste. Garnish with chopped chives or parsley. Makes about 8½ cups (2 L).

TOMATO SOUP

Tomatoes and milk are heated separately, then combined to produce this old fashioned soup. Doesn't freeze well.

Canned tomatoes	14 oz.	398 mL
Milk	2 cups	450 mL
All-purpose flour	1 tbsp.	15 mL
Salt	½ tsp.	2 mL
Pepper	⅛ tsp.	0.5 mL
Granulated sugar	½ tsp.	2 mL
Milk	¼ cup	50 mL
Baking soda	¼ tsp.	1 mL

Heat tomatoes in small saucepan. Break up into small pieces.

Heat first amount of milk in another saucepan.

Mix flour, salt, pepper, sugar and second amount of milk together in small dish until no lumps remain. Stir into simmering milk until it boils and thickens.

Stir baking soda into hot tomatoes. Stir hot tomatoes slowly into hot milk. Makes a generous 3 cups (750 mL).

SMOOTH TOMATO SOUP: Smooth tomatoes in blender before heating.

CREAM OF ZUCCHINI SOUP

This is sure to be your favorite of all the zucchini soups. Equally good with or without cheese.

Butter or margarine	¼ cup	60 mL
Grated zucchini, unpeeled	3 cups	750 mL
Grated carrot	1 cup	250 mL
Chopped onion	¾ cup	175 mL
All-purpose flour	¼ cup	60 mL
Water	2 cups	500 mL
Milk	1 cup	250 mL
Salt	1 tsp.	5 mL
Pepper	¼ tsp.	1 mL
Grated Monterey Jack cheese (optional)	1 cup	250 mL

Melt butter in heavy saucepan. Add zucchini, carrot and onion. Sauté until onion is soft and clear.

Sprinkle with flour and stir well. Add water, milk, salt and pepper. Heat and stir until thickened. Simmer until vegetables are cooked, about 5 minutes.

Add cheese. Stir to melt. Serve. Makes 4½ cups (1.1 L).

Pictured on page 215.

1. Monte Cristo page 185
2. Stew In A Basket page 64
3. Pea Pod Soup page 181
4. Lavosh page 59

PEA SOUP

Made from split green peas. Good choice for a pea soup. Good color. Excellent taste. Freezes well.

Ham bone	1	1
Water	12 cups	2.75 L
Split green peas	3 cups	700 mL
Medium carrots, shredded	3	3
Medium onion, chopped	1	1
Salt	2 tsp.	10 mL
Pepper	½ tsp.	2 mL
Thyme	¼ tsp.	1 mL

Bring ham bone and water to boil. Cover and simmer for about 2 hours. Strain. Measure broth. Add water to bring it up to 12 cups (2.75 L).

Add remaining 6 ingredients. Bring to boil. Cover and simmer at least 1 hour. Peas should be soft and getting mushy. May need a bit of water to thin. Makes about 10 cups (2.25 L).

PEA POD SOUP

A thin broth chock full of vegetables. A different way to use pea pods.

Chicken stock	2 cups	500 mL
Milk	1 cup	250 mL
Chopped carrots	⅓ cup	75 mL
Chopped celery	⅓ cup	75 mL
Finely chopped onion	⅓ cup	75 mL
Salt	¼ tsp.	1 mL
Pepper	⅛ tsp.	0.5 mL
Frozen Chinese pea pods, partially thawed and finely chopped	6 oz.	170 g
Bean sprouts, handful	1	1

Measure first 7 ingredients into saucepan. Bring to boil over medium heat. Boil slowly until vegetables are tender.

Add pea pods and bean sprouts. Bring back to boiling and serve. Makes about 3½ cups (875 mL).

Pictured on page 179.

PEPPER POT SOUP

This extraordinary soup will quickly become a favorite. A large recipe, it freezes well. Excellent.

Water	4 cups	1 L
Chicken bouillon powder	4 tbsp.	60 mL
Good size potatoes, shredded	2	2
Medium carrots, shredded	2	2
Celery stalks, chopped	2	2
Medium onions, chopped	2	2
Green pepper, finely chopped	1	1
All-purpose flour	½ cup	125 mL
Salt	2 tsp.	10 mL
Pepper	½ tsp.	2 mL
Water	1 cup	250 mL
Milk	6 cups	1.5 L

Mix first 7 ingredients together in large saucepan. Bring to boil. Cover and simmer about 20 minutes.

Mix flour, salt, pepper and water together in small container until no lumps remain. Stir into simmering soup to thicken slightly.

Add milk. Heat through. Check for seasoning. Makes about 12½ cups (2.8 L).

CAULIFLOWER CHEESE SOUP

An all round favorite. The best.

Medium head of cauliflower	1	1
Chicken stock	2 cups	500 mL
Butter or margarine	¼ cup	50 mL
Chopped onion	¼ cup	50 mL
All-purpose flour	¼ cup	60 mL
Salt	½ tsp.	2 mL
Pepper	⅛ tsp.	0.5 mL
Milk	2 cups	500 mL
Grated medium Cheddar cheese	1 cup	250 mL
Buttered bread crumbs for garnish		
Parsley		

(continued on next page)

Cook cauliflower in chicken stock until tender. Do not drain. Cool a bit. Run through blender to desired texture. Set aside.

Melt butter in saucepan. Add onion and sauté until limp. Do not brown.

Mix in flour, salt and pepper. Add milk. Heat and stir until it boils and thickens.

Add cheese and cauliflower mixture. Stir to heat and melt cheese. Garnish with buttered bread crumbs. Parsley may be added as an ingredient or as a garnish. Makes about 5 cups (1.25 L).

CREAM OF CAULIFLOWER SOUP: Omit cheese. Excellent.

CAULIFLOWER SOUP: Use water instead of milk.

TUNA BISQUE

This can't be beaten for economy and flavor. You will think you are eating lobster, it is so good.

Chicken stock	2 cups	500 mL
Medium onion, chopped	1	1
Medium potato, chopped	1	1
Chopped celery	1/3 cup	75 mL
Diced carrot	1/3 cup	75 mL
Canned tomatoes, mashed	14 oz.	398 mL
Salt	1 tsp.	5 mL
Pepper	1/4 tsp.	1 mL
Granulated sugar	1 tsp.	2 mL
Milk	2 1/2 cups	600 mL
Milk	1/2 cup	125 mL
All-purpose flour	1/4 cup	50 mL
Canned tuna with juice	6 1/2 oz.	184 g

Combine first 10 ingredients in large saucepan. Bring to a boil over medium heat. Cover and simmer until vegetables are tender.

Mix second amount of milk and flour together until no lumps remain. Stir into simmering soup to thicken.

Add tuna and juice, breaking it up if necessary. Serve hot. Makes about 8 cups (1.75 L).

DENVER SANDWICH

You will find this gratifying any time of day. Also called Western.
Double quantity for a thick sandwich.

Egg	1	1
Water or milk	1 tbsp.	15 mL
Chopped ham	2 tbsp.	30 mL
Finely chopped onion	1 tbsp.	15 mL
Finely chopped green pepper	1 tbsp.	15 mL
Salt, sprinkle		
Pepper, sprinkle		
Toast slices, buttered	2	2

With spoon, beat egg and water together in bowl. Add ham, onion, green pepper, salt and pepper. Pour slowly into hot, well greased frying pan. It will start to cook and won't spread too much. As it cooks, keep drawing to center to keep bread-shape. Brown lightly. Turn to brown other side.

Put between toast slices. Cut and serve hot. Makes 1 serving.

FRANKLY CHEESE BUNS

A boon to the cook to have a different way to serve frankfurters.

Grated Cheddar cheese	1 cup	250 mL
Milk	3 tbsp.	50 mL
Prepared mustard	1 tbsp.	15 mL
Wieners, chopped	3	3
Hot dog buns, uncut	3	3

Heat cheese, milk and mustard in double boiler or heavy saucepan, stirring often, until cheese melts.

Add wieners. Stir to heat through.

Cut a V shaped wedge from each bun. Spoon hot wiener mixture into cavity. May be served as is or broiled until bubbly. Makes 3.

HOT DOG SUPREME: Spread split bun with process cheese. Insert 1 wiener and 2 bacon slices, half cooked. Broil 5 inches (12.5 cm) from heat until sizzling hot. Makes 1.

A sandwich of popular fillings, dipped in egg and grilled.

White bread slices, buttered	3	3
Mozzarella cheese slices	2	2
Cooked ham slice	1	1
Sliced turkey or chicken	1	1
Egg, lightly beaten	1	1
Water	2 tbsp.	30 mL

Layer first bread slice with a slice of cheese, then ham. Top with second bread slice. Put turkey, then remaining cheese on top. Cover with third bread slice.

Mix egg with water. Dip sandwich into egg mixture. Grill in well greased frying pan, browning both sides. Cut diagonally into 4. Makes 1 large serving.

Pictured on page 179.

A golden puff with tomato hidden.

Canned tuna, drained	6½ oz.	184 g
Finely chopped celery	¼ cup	50 mL
Onion powder	⅛ tsp.	0.5 mL
Salt	⅛ tsp.	0.5 mL
Mayonnaise	¼ cup	50 mL
Hamburger buns, split and buttered	3	3
Tomato slices	6	6
Mayonnaise	½ cup	125 mL
Grated Cheddar cheese	¼ cup	60 mL

Mix first 5 ingredients together.

Spread on bun halves.

Top with tomato slice.

Combine mayonnaise with cheese. Spread over all. Broil about 4 inches (10 cm) from heat. Makes 6.

PUMPKIN PIE SQUARES

These have a soft pumpkin top layer over a white cake-like base. Good pumpkin flavor.

FIRST LAYER

Butter or margarine, softened	1 cup	250 mL
Granulated sugar	1 cup	250 mL
Eggs	2	2
Vanilla	1 tsp.	5 mL
All-purpose flour	2 cups	500 mL

SECOND LAYER

Granulated sugar	⅔ cup	150 mL
Salt	1 tsp.	5 mL
Cinnamon	1 tsp.	5 mL
Ginger	½ tsp.	2 mL
Canned pumpkin	14 oz.	398 mL
Milk	1 cup	225 mL
Eggs	2	2

THIRD LAYER

Chopped walnuts	½ cup	125 mL

First Layer: Cream butter and sugar together. Beat in eggs one at a time. Add vanilla.

Add flour. Mix until blended. Spread into greased 9 x 13 inch (22 x 33 cm) pan. Set aside.

Second Layer: Measure all ingredients into mixing bowl. Beat together until blended. Pour over top of first layer. Bake in 400°F (220°C) oven for 10 minutes. Reduce heat to 325°F (150°C) and continue to bake for 40 to 50 minutes until set.

Third Layer: About 5 minutes before removing from oven, sprinkle top layer with nuts. When cool cut into 54 squares.

Pictured on page 197.

Paré Pointer

She plans to get rich if she eats enough fortune cookies.

A chewy firm square. Good flavor.

FIRST LAYER

Whole wheat flour	1½ cups	350 mL
Rolled oats	1 cup	250 mL
Wheat germ	½ cup	125 mL
Brown sugar, packed	½ cup	125 mL
Sesame seeds	2 tbsp.	30 mL
Salt	½ tsp.	2 mL
Egg yolk	1	1
Butter or margarine, melted	½ cup	125 mL
Rolled oats	1 cup	250 mL
Sesame seeds	2 tbsp.	30 mL

SECOND LAYER

Butter or margarine	⅓ cup	75 mL
Honey	⅓ cup	75 mL
Egg white	1	1
Brown sugar, packed	½ cup	125 mL
Raisins	⅓ cup	75 mL
Coconut	⅓ cup	75 mL
Chopped peanuts or walnuts	⅓ cup	75 mL
Vanilla	1 tsp.	5 mL

First Layer: Measure first 6 ingredients into bowl. Mix. Stir egg yolk into cooled butter and add. Mix well. Press very firmly into greased 9 x 13 inch (22 x 33 cm) pan. Bake in 350° F (180° C) oven for 10 minutes.

Along with first layer place second amount of rolled oats and sesame seeds in a pan in oven to bake for 10 minutes also.

Second Layer: In large saucepan melt butter. Remove from heat. Stir in honey and egg white. Add all remaining ingredients along with rolled oats and sesame seeds that were baked for 10 minutes. Press this layer over first layer. Bake in 350° F (180° C) oven for 20 minutes. Cuts into 54 squares.

Pictured on page 197.

CHERRY CHEWS

Rich and chewy. Easy to make.

BOTTOM LAYER

Butter or margarine	½ cup	125 mL
All-purpose flour	1 cup	250 mL
Rolled oats	1 cup	225 mL
Brown sugar, packed	1 cup	225 mL
Baking powder	1 tsp.	5 mL
Salt	½ tsp.	2 mL

TOP LAYER

Eggs	2	2
Brown sugar, packed	1 cup	225 mL
Almond flavoring	½ tsp.	2 mL
Coconut	1 cup	225 mL
All-purpose flour	2 tbsp.	30 mL
Baking powder	1 tsp.	5 mL
Salt	¼ tsp.	1 mL
Glazed cherries, cut up	1 cup	250 mL
Pecans, coarsely chopped	½ cup	125 mL

Bottom Layer: Mix all 6 ingredients together until mealy. Pack into ungreased 9 x 13 inch (22 x 33 cm) pan. Bake in 350° F (180° C) oven for 10 minutes.

Top Layer: Beat eggs with spoon. Add remaining ingredients in order given. Spoon over bottom layer. Bake in 350° F (180° C) oven for 25 to 30 minutes, until set. Frost if desired. Cuts into 54 squares.

ICING

Icing (confectioner's) sugar	2 cups	500 mL
Butter or margarine, softened	3 tbsp.	50 mL
Almond flavoring	½ tsp.	2 mL
Cherry juice or water	2 tbsp.	30 mL

Beat all together adding more liquid if needed for easy spreading. Cherry juice makes a light pink icing and water makes a white icing. Spread over top.

Pictured on page 197.

This is an exceptionally good square. With its caramel taste and lots of nuts, there isn't anyone who doesn't like it.

Butter or margarine	¼ cup	50 mL
Brown sugar, packed	1 cup	225 mL
Egg, beaten	1	1
Chopped walnuts	½ cup	125 mL
All-purpose flour	¾ cup	175 mL
Baking powder	1 tsp.	5 mL
Salt	¼ tsp.	1 mL
Medium-grind coconut	1 cup	200 mL

Melt butter in large saucepan. Remove from heat. Add sugar. Stir in beaten egg. Measure in nuts, flour, baking powder, salt and coconut. Stir well. Scrape into greased 9 x 9 inch (22 x 22 cm) pan. Bake in 350° F (180° C) oven for 30 minutes or until set and a medium brown. Frost when cool with caramel icing.

ICING

Butter or margarine	¼ cup	50 mL
Brown sugar, packed	½ cup	125 mL
Milk	2 tbsp.	30 mL
Icing (confectioner's) sugar	1 cup	250 mL

Combine butter, sugar and milk in saucepan. Bring to boil and simmer 2 minutes. Cool. To speed up this procedure, run some cold water in the sink. Set pan in water. Stir until cool.

Stir in icing sugar. If too stiff, add a bit more milk until soft enough to spread. Smooth over bars. Cut when set. Yields 36 squares.

Did you know that a unicorn belongs to the female sex? It is a Myth.

CHOCOLATE CRISPY NUT SQUARES

Crisp rice cereal squares with a chocolate and nutty flavor.

Butter or margarine	⅓ cup	75 mL
Corn syrup or honey	⅓ cup	75 mL
Cocoa	½ cup	125 mL
Tiny marshmallows	3 cups	700 mL
Vanilla	1 tsp.	5 mL
Crisp rice cereal	4 cups	900 mL
Peanuts or your favorite nuts	1 cup	250 mL

Combine first 5 ingredients in large saucepan. Melt and stir over low heat until smooth. Remove from heat.

Stir in cereal and nuts. Pack into greased 9 x 9 inch (22 x 22 cm) pan. Let stand. Cuts into 36 squares.

Pictured on page 197.

CARAMEL TOFFEE SQUARES

There is a layer of caramel under that chocolate. When freezing, allow time to thaw before cutting.

BOTTOM LAYER

All-purpose flour	1¼ cups	300 mL
Granulated sugar	¼ cup	50 mL
Butter, softened	½ cup	125 mL
More butter	2 tsp.	10 mL

SECOND LAYER

Butter	½ cup	125 mL
Brown sugar, packed	½ cup	125 mL
Corn syrup	2 tbsp.	30 mL
Sweetened condensed milk	½ cup	125 mL

THIRD LAYER

Semisweet chocolate chips	2 cups	450 mL

(continued on next page)

Bottom Layer: Crumble first 4 ingredients well. Pack into ungreased 9 x 9 inch (22 x 22 cm) pan. Bake in 350°F (180°C) oven for 20 minutes.

Second Layer: Combine next 4 ingredients in heavy saucepan. Bring to boil over medium heat. Boil 5 minutes, stirring constantly as it burns easily. Remove from heat. Beat with spoon slowly until it shows signs of thickening. Pour over bottom layer.

Third Layer: Melt chocolate in saucepan over low heat or over hot water. Pour over second layer. Chill. Cut into 36 squares.

CHOCOLATE REVEL BARS

A scrumptious square, chewy with a smooth chocolate center. Makes a large batch.

Butter or margarine, softened	1 cup	250 mL
Brown sugar, packed	2 cups	500 mL
Eggs	2	2
Vanilla	2 tsp.	10 mL
All-purpose flour	2½ cups	625 mL
Baking soda	1 tsp.	5 mL
Salt	1 tsp.	5 mL
Rolled oats	3 cups	750 mL
Sweetened condensed milk	11 oz.	300 mL
Semisweet chocolate chips	2 cups	500 mL
Butter or margarine	2 tbsp.	30 mL
Vanilla	2 tsp.	10 mL
Salt	½ tsp.	2 mL
Chopped nuts	1 cup	250 mL

Cream butter and sugar together well. Beat in eggs and vanilla.

Add flour, baking soda and salt. Mix in. Add rolled oats. Stir together. Press ⅔ mixture into greased 10 x 15 inch (25 x 38 cm) pan. Set aside.

In heavy pot or top of double boiler combine milk, chocolate chips, butter, vanilla and salt. When chips are melted stir in nuts. Spoon over prepared base. Spread evenly. Sprinkle with remaining ⅓ oatmeal mixture. Bake in 350°F (180°C) oven for about 20 minutes or until browned. Cuts into 70 squares.

Pictured on page 197.

NUT SMACKS

Butterscotch flavor, rich with nuts and brown sugar.

Brown sugar, packed	½ cup	125 mL
Egg yolks	2	2
Vanilla	1 tsp.	5 mL
Butter or margarine, softened	½ cup	125 mL
Salt	¼ tsp.	1 mL
All-purpose flour	1½ cups	350 mL
Baking powder	1 tsp.	5 mL
Egg whites	2	2
Brown sugar, packed	1 cup	225 mL
Chopped walnuts	1 cup	225 mL

First Layer: Crumble first 7 ingredients together well in large bowl. Press firmly into 9 x 9 inch (22 x 22 cm) ungreased pan. Set aside.

Second Layer: Beat egg whites until frothy. Add second amount of brown sugar ⅓ at a time, beating until stiff. Fold in nuts. Spoon over unbaked base, spreading evenly. Bake in 350°F (180°C) oven for about 25 minutes until golden. Cool. Cut with sharp knife, dipped in hot water between cuts. Covering pan allows meringue to soften for easier cutting. Makes 36 squares.

SAUCEPAN BROWNIES

At last, a brownie that you can make on a day which is too hot to think about food. It has an exceptionally rich chocolate flavor.

Semisweet chocolate chips	2⅔ cups	650 mL
Evaporated milk	1 cup	250 mL
Vanilla wafer crumbs	3 cups	750 mL
Tiny marshmallows	2 cups	500 mL
Chopped walnuts	1 cup	250 mL
Icing (confectioner's) sugar	1 cup	250 mL
Salt	½ tsp.	2 mL
Chocolate mixture saved from above	½ cup	125 mL
Evaporated milk	2 tsp.	10 mL

(continued on next page)

Put chips and milk into large saucepan. Melt over medium-low heat until chips combine when stirred. Remove from heat. Measure out ½ cup (125 mL) and set aside for final step.

Stir crumbs, marshmallows, nuts, icing sugar and salt into remaining chocolate mixture in saucepan. Press into 9 x 9 inch (22 x 22 cm) greased pan or line it with waxed paper.

To the reserved chocolate mixture stir in 2 tsp. (10 mL) evaporated milk. Spread evenly over brownies. Chill and cut into 36 squares.

NEAPOLITAN SQUARES

Delicate looking, a good keeper and an attractive addition to a plate of squares.

Graham cracker crumbs	1¼ cups	300 mL
Butter or margarine, melted	½ cup	125 mL
Brown sugar, packed	½ cup	125 mL
All-purpose flour	⅓ cup	75 mL
Medium-grind coconut	2 cups	450 mL
Sweetened condensed milk	11 oz.	300 mL

Bottom Layer: Combine first 4 ingredients. Press into 9 x 9 inch (22 x 22 cm) pan with greased sides. This makes it easier to remove side pieces. Bake in 350° F (180° C) oven for 10 minutes.

Second Layer: In clean bowl, combine coconut with condensed milk. Spread over bottom layer. Bake in 350° F (180° C) oven for 20 minutes or until a very slight tinge of light brown begins to show on the edges. Allow to cool before frosting.

ICING

Icing (confectioner's) sugar	2 cups	500 mL
Butter or margarine	4 tbsp.	50 mL
Maraschino cherry juice	3 tbsp.	50 mL

Beat all together, adding a bit more juice, if needed, to make icing soft enough to spread. Spread over cooled bars. Cover tightly and store at least a day to soften. Can be used the same day as baked but it is more difficult to cut. If you do not have any cherry juice, use water with a bit of red food coloring with ¼ tsp. (1 mL) cherry or almond flavoring. Cut into 36 squares.

BUTTERSCOTCH CONFETTI

This freezes so well for so long, there is no excuse not to have it on hand; that is, of course, if you keep it hidden.

Butter or margarine	¼ cup	50 mL
Peanut butter	½ cup	125 mL
Butterscotch chips	1 cup	250 mL
Small colored marshmallows (bag)	8 oz.	250 g

Melt butter and peanut butter in a large saucepan over low heat. Stir in chips until melted. Cool until you can hold your hand on bottom of pot. To speed process, stir while holding pan in cold water until cool enough. Add marshmallows and stir until all are coated. Pack down in 9 x 9 inch (22 x 22 cm) pan that has been lined with waxed paper. Refrigerate. Cut into 36 squares.

Variation: To above ingredients add ½ cup (125 mL) chopped walnuts and/or ½ cup (125 mL) medium coconut.

CHOCOLATE CHIP SQUARES

This is a moist, caramel-tasting square, with the chocolate flavor giving it the extra touch.

Butter or margarine, softened	½ cup	125 mL
Brown sugar, packed	½ cup	125 mL
Granulated sugar	¼ cup	50 mL
Egg	1	1
Vanilla	1 tsp.	5 mL
All-purpose flour	1 cup	250 mL
Baking soda	½ tsp.	3 mL
Salt	½ tsp.	2 mL
Semisweet chocolate chips	1 cup	225 mL
Chopped walnuts	½ cup	125 mL

In medium size bowl, cream butter with brown sugar. Add white sugar and cream again. Add egg and vanilla and beat well. Measure in flour, soda and salt. Stir until well blended. Add chips and nuts stirring to combine. Scrape into greased 9 x 9 inch (22 x 22 cm) pan. Bake in 350°F (180°C) oven for 25 to 30 minutes until set and a nice brown color. When cool cut into 36 squares.

CHOCOLATE BARS

A good imitation of a popular candy bar, this is chocolate with a bit of a crunch.

Butter or margarine	⅓ cup	75 mL
Semisweet chocolate chips	1 cup	250 mL
Large marshmallows	35	35
Salted peanuts	1 cup	250 mL
Crisp rice cereal	2 cups	500 mL

Melt butter, chocolate chips and marshmallows in large heavy saucepan.

Stir in peanuts and cereal. Spread in foil-lined 8 x 8 inch (20 x 20 cm) pan. Chill. Cut into 25 squares.

Pictured on page 197.

PEANUT BUTTER SQUARES

Just like a candy bar and so easy.

Butter or margarine	1 cup	250 mL
Smooth peanut butter	1 cup	250 mL
Icing (confectioner's) sugar	2½ cups	625 mL
Graham cracker crumbs	1½ cups	375 mL
Semisweet chocolate chips	1⅓ cups	325 mL

In medium saucepan, melt butter and peanut butter.

Stir in icing sugar and graham cracker crumbs. Press into ungreased 9 x 13 inch (22 x 33 cm) pan. Set aside.

Melt chocolate chips in heavy saucepan over low heat. Stir to blend. Spread over top. Cool. Cuts into 54 squares.

Pictured on page 197.

FRUITCAKE SQUARES

Fruity and good. A snap to make.

Butter or margarine, softened	¼ cup	50 mL
Egg	1	1
Sweetened condensed milk	⅔ cup	150 mL
Vanilla	1 tsp.	5 mL
Canned applesauce	14 oz.	398 mL
All-purpose flour	1½ cups	375 mL
Baking powder	2 tsp.	10 mL
Salt	½ tsp.	2 mL
Chopped red candied cherries	⅓ cup	75 mL
Chopped green candied cherries	⅓ cup	75 mL
Chopped dates	⅓ cup	75 mL
Raisins	⅓ cup	75 mL
Chopped nuts	⅓ cup	75 mL

Beat butter and egg together. Mix in condensed milk, vanilla and applesauce.

Measure in remaining ingredients in order given. Stir well to mix thoroughly. Spread into greased 9 x 9 inch (22 x 22 cm) pan. Bake in 325° F (160° C) oven for about 35 to 45 minutes. Cuts into 36 squares.

Pictured on page 197.

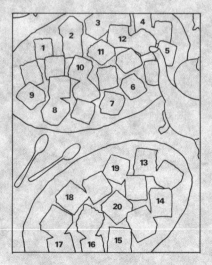

Not only is this the easiest and fastest brownie to make, it is also the best tasting ever.

Butter or margarine	½ **cup**	**125 mL**
Cocoa	¼ **cup**	**50 mL**
Eggs	**2**	**2**
Granulated sugar	**1 cup**	**225 mL**
All-purpose flour	¾ **cup**	**175 mL**
Chopped walnuts	½ **cup**	**125 mL**
Salt	⅛ **tsp.**	**0.5 mL**

In small saucepan melt butter and cocoa, stirring as it melts. Remove from heat.

In medium size bowl beat eggs until frothy. Add sugar, flour, nuts and salt. Don't stir yet. Pour cocoa mixture over top and stir all together. Scrape batter into greased 8 x 8 inch (20 x 20 cm) pan. Bake in 350°F (180°C) oven for about 30 minutes until the edges begin to show signs of pulling away from the sides of the pan. Cut into 25 squares when cool. Frost for a more festive occasion.

ICING

Icing (confectioner's) sugar	1⅓ **cups**	**300 mL**
Cocoa	⅓ **cup**	**75 mL**
Butter or margarine, softened	3 **tbsp.**	**50 mL**
Hot coffee or water	5 **tsp.**	**25 mL**

Beat all together, adding more liquid if mixture is too firm to spread easily. Spread over baked brownies. Allow to set before cutting. For a glossy look, frost while brownies are still warm.

Paré Pointer

No one talks more than moths. They are always chewing the rag.

NOODLE SQUARES

A butterscotch noodle topping covers a middle layer of chocolate. Good.

Butter or margarine	½ cup	125 mL
Brown sugar, packed	¼ cup	60 mL
All-purpose flour	1 cup	250 mL
Semisweet chocolate chips	1 cup	250 mL
Light cream	½ cup	125 mL
Smooth peanut butter	1 cup	250 mL
Brown sugar, packed	½ cup	125 mL
Tiny marshmallows	5 cups	1.25 L
Chow mein noodles	4 cups	1 L

Mix butter, first amount of brown sugar and flour together until crumbly. Press into 9 x 13 inch (22 x 33 cm) pan. Bake in 350°F (180°C) oven for 15 minutes.

Immediately sprinkle chocolate chips over top. When they melt, spread evenly. Chill.

Combine cream, peanut butter, second amount of brown sugar and marshmallows together in large saucepan. Melt, stirring often, over medium heat.

Add noodles to melted mixture. Stir and spread over firm chocolate layer. Chill. Cuts into 54 squares.

Pictured on page 197.

CRISPY CHIP SQUARES

Textured like shortbread. Similar to a chocolate chip cookie with a caramel taste.

Butter or margarine, softened	1 cup	250 mL
Brown sugar, packed	1 cup	250 mL
Vanilla	1 tsp.	5 mL
Salt	¼ tsp.	1 mL
All-purpose flour	2 cups	500 mL
Semisweet chocolate chips	1 cup	250 mL
Chopped pecans	1 cup	250 mL

(continued on next page)

Cream butter and sugar together well. Mix in vanilla and salt. Add flour. Mix together well.

Add chips and pecans. Work into dough. Press into ungreased 9 x 13 inch (22 x 33 cm) pan. Bake in 350° F (180° C) oven for about 25 minutes. These turn quite crisp when cold so they must be cut while warm. Cuts into 54 squares.

Pictured on page 197.

MATRIMONIAL SQUARES

Favorite date squares that are not nearly as messy to eat as some others. These crumbs hold together well.

CRUMB LAYERS

All-purpose flour	1¼ cups	300 mL
Rolled oats	1½ cups	375 mL
Brown sugar, packed	1 cup	250 mL
Baking soda	1 tsp.	5 mL
Salt	½ tsp.	2 mL
Butter or margarine	1 cup	250 mL

FILLING

Dates, cut up	½ lb.	250 g
Granulated sugar	½ cup	125 mL
Water	⅔ cup	150 mL

Crumb Layers: Measure flour, oats, sugar, soda, salt and butter into large bowl. Cut butter into the ingredients until crumbly. Press a large ½ to ⅔ of crumbs into greased 9 x 9 inch (22 x 22 cm) pan.

Filling: In saucepan combine dates, sugar and water. Bring to boil and allow to simmer until mushy. If mixture becomes too dry before dates have softened enough, add more water. If you find you have too much water, don't worry. Just keep simmering until some has been boiled away. Spread over bottom layer of crumbs. Sprinkle remaining crumbs over top. Press down with your hand. Bake in 350° F (180° C) oven for 30 minutes until a rich golden brown color. If you are in a great hurry and your butter is hard as a rock, you can still make this using melted butter. It will be more difficult to spread the top crumbs. Cut into 36 squares.

GRANT'S SPECIAL

Otherwise known as Seafoam Chews. His friend's mother made this "really good square" so what else could I do?

FIRST LAYER

Butter or margarine, softened	½ cup	125 mL
Granulated sugar	½ cup	125 mL
Brown sugar, packed	½ cup	125 mL
All-purpose flour	2 cups	500 mL
Baking powder	2 tsp.	10 mL
Salt	½ tsp.	2 mL
Baking soda	1 tsp.	5 mL
Egg yolks	2	2
Milk	3 tbsp.	50 mL
Vanilla	1 tsp.	5 mL

SECOND LAYER

Semisweet chocolate chips	1 cup	225 mL

THIRD LAYER

Egg whites	2	2
Brown sugar, packed	1 cup	225 mL

FOURTH LAYER

Salted peanuts, chopped	¾ cup	175 mL

First Layer: Measure first 10 ingredients into large bowl. Crumble together well. Press into ungreased 9 x 9 inch (22 x 22 cm) pan at least 2 inches (5 cm) deep. This is a higher square than most.

Second Layer: Sprinkle chips over top of first layer.

Third Layer: Beat egg whites until frothy. Add second amount of sugar ⅓ at a time, beating until stiff. Spread over top of chips.

Fourth Layer: Sprinkle peanuts over top of the beaten egg white, pressing lightly as they tend to fall off when baked. Bake in 350° F (180° C) oven for 35 minutes. Cool. Cover to soften meringue for easy cutting into 36 squares.

Paré Pointer

Several dentists working together are better known as a drill team.

With the pineapple and touch of rum, this is well named.

BOTTOM LAYER

Butter or margarine	½ cup	125 mL
Granulated sugar	¼ cup	50 mL
All-purpose flour	1¼ cups	300 mL

TOP LAYER

Eggs	2	2
Brown sugar, packed	1 cup	225 mL
Crushed pineapple, drained (save juice for icing)	½ cup	125 mL
Coconut	1 cup	225 mL
Candied cherries, chopped	⅓ cup	75 mL
Rum flavoring	1 tsp.	5 mL
All-purpose flour	2 tbsp.	30 mL
Baking powder	½ tsp.	2 mL

Bottom Layer: Crumble butter, sugar and flour together well. Pack into 9 x 9 inch (22 x 22 cm) ungreased pan. Bake in 350° F (180° C) oven for 15 minutes.

Top Layer: Beat eggs slightly. Stir in remaining ingredients. Spread over bottom layer. Bake in 350° F (180° C) oven for 25 to 30 minutes until a medium brown color and is set. Frost with icing below. Cut into 36 squares.

ICING

Icing (confectioner's) sugar	1½ cups	350 mL
Butter or margarine	3 tbsp.	50 mL
Rum flavoring	½ tsp.	2 mL
Pineapple juice	5 tsp.	25 mL

Combine all together in bowl. Beat, adding more juice if icing is too stiff. Spread over bars. Allow to set before cutting.

Paré Pointer

Talk about being faithful! Once a tick finds a friend it sticks to him.

NANAIMO BARS

A special occasion brings this to mind. You can make it the day before or even have it in the freezer.

BOTTOM LAYER

Butter or margarine	½ cup	125 mL
Granulated sugar	¼ cup	50 mL
Cocoa	5 tbsp.	75 mL
Egg, beaten	1	1
Graham cracker crumbs	1¾ cups	400 mL
Fine coconut (or medium)	¾ cup	175 mL
Walnuts, finely chopped	½ cup	125 mL

SECOND LAYER

Butter or margarine, softened	½ cup	125 mL
Milk	3 tbsp.	50 mL
Vanilla custard powder	2 tbsp.	30 mL
Icing (confectioner's) sugar	2 cups	500 mL

THIRD LAYER

Semisweet chocolate chips (or 4 squares semisweet chocolate)	⅔ cup	150 mL
Butter or margarine	2 tbsp.	30 mL

Bottom Layer: Melt first 3 ingredients in top of double boiler or in heavy saucepan. Add beaten egg and stir to cook and thicken. Remove from heat. Stir in crumbs, coconut and nuts. Press firmly into ungreased 9 x 9 inch (22 x 22 cm) pan.

Second Layer: Cream butter, milk, custard powder and icing sugar together well. Beat until light. Spread over bottom layer.

Third Layer: Melt chips and butter over low heat. Cool. When cool but still runny, spread over second layer. Chill in refrigerator. Use a sharp knife to cut 36 squares.

Note: Vanilla pudding and pie filling (not instant) may be used in place of custard powder.

Paré Pointer

One way to get a soggy noodle is to wash your hair too much.

A really scrumptious square. No need to use the oven. If you happen to be a little short of nuts, coconut or cherries, you can vary the quantities without anyone knowing it wasn't meant to be that way.

Whole graham crackers

Brown sugar, packed	1 cup	250 mL
Butter or margarine	½ cup	125 mL
Milk	½ cup	125 mL
Graham cracker crumbs	1⅓ cups	325 mL
Chopped walnuts	1 cup	250 mL
Shredded or medium coconut	1 cup	250 mL
Maraschino cherries, cut and well-drained	¼ cup	50 mL

Line ungreased 9 x 9 inch (22 x 22 cm) pan with whole crackers trimming to fit. Set aside.

In saucepan combine sugar, butter and milk. Bring to boil. Simmer for 2 minutes. Remove from heat.

Add cracker crumbs, nuts, coconut and cherries stirring to mix. Pour over crackers in pan. Cool. Frost and let stand overnight.

ICING

Icing (confectioner's) sugar	1½ cups	350 mL
Butter or margarine	3 tbsp.	50 mL
Milk	5 tsp.	25 mL
Vanilla	½ tsp.	3 mL
Red food coloring		

Beat all together in small bowl adjusting liquid if required, and adding enough color to tint a pretty pink. Ice bars and allow to stand for several hours. Cut into 36 squares.

Paré Pointer

Talk about a language barrier! We sing "amen" instead of "awomen". That's because we sing hymns not hers.

CHOCOLATE OAT SQUARES

There is a hint of both peanut butter and chocolate in these crunchy crisp squares.

Butter or margarine	1 cup	250 mL
Brown sugar, packed	½ cup	125 mL
Granulated sugar	½ cup	125 mL
Rolled oats	3 cups	750 mL
Smooth peanut butter	½ cup	125 mL
Semisweet chocolate chips	½ cup	125 mL
Water	2 tbsp.	30 mL

Melt butter in large saucepan. Stir in both sugars and rolled oats. Press into ungreased 9 x 13 inch (22 x 33 cm) pan. Bake in 350°F (180°C) oven for about 15 minutes until lightly browned. Cool. Spread cooled squares with peanut butter.

Melt chips with water in small saucepan. Stir often. Spread over peanut butter. Chill. Cuts into 36 squares.

Pictured on page 197.

MILLIONAIRE SQUARES

Millionaire means rich and that is exactly what these squares are.

BOTTOM LAYER

Oatmeal cookies, crushed (Dads or similar)	2 cups	500 mL
Melted butter or margarine	½ cup	125 mL

FILLING

Semisweet chocolate squares (or ½ cup, 125 mL, chips)	3	3
Butter or margarine	½ cup	125 mL
Egg	1	1
Icing (confectioner's) sugar	2 cups	450 mL
Chopped walnuts (optional)	½ cup	125 mL
Reserved crumbs for topping		

(continued on next page)

Bottom Layer: Combine crushed or ground crumbs with melted butter. Measure ¼ cup (50 mL) crumbs and set aside for topping. Press remaining crumbs into ungreased 8 x 8 inch (20 x 20 cm) pan. Bake in 350° F (180° C) oven for 5 minutes. Cool. This baking step can be omitted if you make crust ahead and allow it to stand a few hours to harden and dry.

Filling: Melt chocolate and butter over low heat. Remove from heat. Add egg and beat. Add icing sugar beating until smooth. Add walnuts. Mix. If too soft to hold shape, add ¼ cup (50 mL) more icing sugar. This will set up a bit when chilled but not much more than when you spread it in the pan. When the crust is baked, you will find that the filling is much easier to spread without the crumbs lifting to follow your spoon. After filling is smoothed over the crust, sprinkle with reserved crumbs. Refrigerate. Cut into 36 small squares or 25 larger.

BANANA CHIP BARS

Moist and flavorful.

Butter or margarine	½ cup	125 mL
Graham cracker crumbs	2 cups	500 mL
Granulated sugar	¼ cup	50 mL
Sweetened condensed milk	11 oz.	300 mL
Mashed banana, about 3	1 cup	250 mL
Flaked coconut	1⅓ cups	325 mL
Semisweet chocolate chips	1 cup	250 mL
Chopped pecans or walnuts	1 cups	250 mL

Melt butter in saucepan. Stir in crumbs and sugar. Press into greased 9 x 13 inch (22 x 33 cm) pan.

Mix condensed milk and banana together. Pour over top. Spread evenly.

Sprinkle with coconut, then with chocolate chips followed by pecans. Press down all over with your hand. Bake in 350° F (180° C) oven until browned, about 25 to 30 minutes. Chill. Cuts into 54 squares.

Pictured on page 197.

NUTTY CHIP SQUARES

These thick chewy squares are chocolaty and nutty.

BOTTOM LAYER

All-purpose flour	1 cup	250 mL
Brown sugar, packed	1 cup	250 mL
Rolled oats	½ cup	125 mL
Coconut	½ cup	125 mL
Baking soda	1 tsp.	5 mL
Butter or margarine, softened	½ cup	125 mL

TOP LAYER

Eggs	2	2
Brown sugar, packed	½ cup	125 mL
All-purpose flour	1 tbsp.	15 mL
Semisweet chocolate chips	1 cup	250 mL
Chopped walnuts	½ cup	125 mL
Butter or margarine, melted	¼ cup	60 mL

Bottom Layer: Combine all ingredients in bowl. Mix until crumbly. Press into ungreased 9 x 9 inch (22 x 22 cm) pan. Set aside.

Top Layer: Beat eggs until frothy. Add sugar and flour. Stir. Add chips, nuts and melted butter. Stir well and pour over bottom layer. Bake in 350°F (180°C) oven for 30 to 35 minutes. Cuts into 36 squares.

Pictured on page 197.

CHEESECAKE SQUARES

A crisp butterscotch base topped with a cheesecake layer.

BOTTOM LAYER

Butterscotch chips	1 cup	250 mL
Butter or margarine	⅓ cup	75 mL
Graham cracker crumbs	1½ cups	375 mL

TOP LAYER

Cream cheese, softened	8 oz.	250 g
Granulated sugar	⅓ cup	75 mL
Eggs	2	2
All-purpose flour	2 tbsp.	30 mL
Lemon juice	3 tbsp.	50 mL

(continued on next page)

Bottom Layer: Melt chips and butter in saucepan over low heat. Stir in crumbs. Reserve ½ cup (125 mL). Press remaining crumbs into ungreased 9 x 9 inch (22 x 22 cm) pan. Bake in 325°F (160°C) oven for 12 minutes. Cool.

Top Layer: Beat cheese and sugar together. Beat in eggs 1 at a time. Add flour. Mix. Add lemon juice. Spread over bottom layer. Sprinkle with reserved crumbs. Bake in 325°F (160°C) oven for 20 to 25 minutes. Cool well. Cuts into 36 squares.

Pictured on page 197.

CHERRY CRISP SQUARES

Like a chewy shortbread. Colorful.

Butter or margarine, softened	1 cup	250 mL
More butter or margarine	2 tbsp.	30 mL
Brown sugar	1 cup	250 mL
All-purpose flour	2½ cups	625 mL
Chopped candied cherries	1 cup	250 mL
Finely chopped almonds	⅔ cup	150 mL

Cream butter and sugar well. Slowly beat in flour. Mix well.

Add cherries and almonds. Beat well. Turn into ungreased 9 x 9 inch (22 x 22 cm) pan. Bake in 325°F (160°C) oven for 30 to 35 minutes until golden. Ice when cool.

ICING

Butter or margarine, softened	3 tbsp.	50 mL
Icing (confectioner's) sugar	1½ cups	375 mL
Maraschino cherry juice	2½ tbsp.	35 mL

Beat all together. Cherry flavoring and water may be used in place of juice along with a bit of red food coloring. Add more juice for easy spreading. Spread over cooled layer. Cut into 36 squares.

Pictured on page 197.

CHERRY CHOCOLATE SQUARES

An exquisite no-bake square. It has a chocolate base and top with a cherry center. So pretty. So special.

BOTTOM LAYER

Butter or margarine	½ cup	125 mL
Granulated sugar	¼ cup	50 mL
Cocoa	⅓ cup	75 mL
Egg, beaten	1	1
Graham cracker crumbs	1¾ cups	400 mL
Coconut	½ cup	125 mL
Walnuts, finely chopped	⅓ cup	75 mL
Water	1 tbsp.	15 mL

SECOND LAYER

Butter or margarine, softened	¼ cup	60 mL
Maraschino cherry juice	2 tbsp.	30 mL
Almond flavoring	1 tsp.	5 mL
Icing (confectioner's) sugar	2 cups	500 mL
Chopped maraschino cherries	⅓ cup	75 mL

THIRD LAYER

Butter or margarine	2 tbsp.	30 mL
Chocolate chips	⅓ cup	75 mL

Bottom Layer: Put butter, sugar and cocoa into heavy saucepan over medium heat. When melted, stir in fork beaten egg and cook until thickened slightly. Remove from heat. Stir in crumbs, coconut, walnuts and water. Press very firmly into ungreased 9 x 9 inch (22 x 22 cm) pan.

Second Layer: Beat butter, cherry juice, almond flavoring and icing sugar together well. Beat slowly at first to keep sugar from flying all over. Blot cherries with paper towels and stir in. Drop dabs here and there over first layer then spread. Let stand for 10 minutes or so. Using your hand, pat smooth.

Third Layer: Melt butter in small saucepan. Add chocolate chips and stir to melt. Pour over top of second layer. With teaspoon, smooth over all. Work quickly so as not to bring any second layer up to the top. Chill. Cuts into 36 squares.

BLUEBERRY CHEESE SQUARES

A sure fire hit. Like a tiny cheesecake you can hold in your hand.

FIRST LAYER

Butter or margarine	½ cup	125 mL
Graham cracker crumbs	1¾ cups	425 mL
Granulated sugar	¼ cup	50 mL

SECOND LAYER

Cream cheese, softened	8 oz.	250 g
Granulated sugar	½ cup	125 mL
Eggs	2	2
Vanilla	1 tsp.	5 mL

FILLING

Blueberry pie filling	19 oz.	540 mL
Cornstarch	1 tbsp.	15 mL
Water	2 tbsp.	30 mL
Whipping cream (or 1 env. topping)	1 cup	250 mL
Granulated sugar	1 tbsp.	15 mL
Vanilla	½ tsp.	2 mL

First Layer: Melt butter in medium size saucepan over low heat. Stir in graham crumbs and sugar. Pack into ungreased 9 x 13 inch (22 x 33 cm) pan. Set aside.

Second Layer: Beat cheese and sugar together. Beat in eggs 1 at a time. Add vanilla. Mix well. Spread over first layer. Bake in 350° F (180° C) oven for 15 to 20 minutes. Chill well or partially freeze.

Filling: Put filling into saucepan. Heat until it simmers. Stir often.

Mix cornstarch and water together. Stir into blueberry filling until it boils and thickens. Cool well. This can be hastened by placing saucepan in cold water in sink. When cold, spread over first layer. Use all of filling or just part of it to make the thickness you would like.

Topping: Whip cream, sugar and vanilla until stiff. Spread over second layer. Cuts into 36 squares.

Pictured on page 197.

CHOCOLATE MINT SQUARES

A good flavor combination. No baking required.

Evaporated milk (or light cream)	½ cup	125 mL
Semisweet chocolate chips	1 cup	250 mL
Vanilla	½ tsp.	2 mL
Graham cracker crumbs	2 cups	500 mL
Icing (confectioner's) sugar	½ cup	125 mL
Chopped walnuts	½ cup	125 mL

Put milk, chips and vanilla into large saucepan over low heat. Stir often to hasten melting. Remove from heat.

Add cracker crumbs, sugar and nuts. Stir together until mixed well. Pack into greased 9 x 9 inch (22 x 22 cm) pan. Frost with Mint Icing.

MINT ICING

Icing (confectioner's) sugar	2 cups	500 mL
Butter or margarine	¼ cup	60 mL
Peppermint flavoring	1 tsp.	5 mL
Water or milk	2 tbsp.	30 mL

Beat all ingredients together until smooth adding more liquid if needed for easy spreading. Spread over pan contents. Chill well.

GLAZE

Butter or margarine	2 tbsp.	30 mL
Semisweet chocolate chips	⅓ cup	75 mL

Melt butter in small saucepan. Add chips and stir to melt. Quickly smooth with back of spoon over top. Chill. Cuts into 36 squares.

Pictured on page 197.

Paré Pointer

She gets so excited she is like a pin — pointed in one direction and headed in another.

CHERRY SQUARES

This is one of the most popular bar-type cookies. After you've tried it you will understand why.

FIRST LAYER

All-purpose flour	1¼ cups	300 mL
Brown sugar, packed	⅓ cup	75 mL
Butter or margarine	½ cup	125 mL

SECOND LAYER

Eggs	2	2
Brown sugar, packed	1¼ cups	275 mL
All-purpose flour	1 tbsp.	15 mL
Baking powder	½ tsp.	2 mL
Salt	⅛ tsp.	0.5 mL
Medium-grind coconut	1 cup	225 mL
Chopped walnuts	½ cup	125 mL
Candied or maraschino cherries, cut up	½ cup	125 mL

First Layer: Crumble first 3 ingredients together well. Press into ungreased 9 x 9 inch (22 x 22 cm) pan. Bake in 350°F (180°C) oven for 15 minutes.

Second Layer: Beat eggs slightly and add the rest of the ingredients in order given. Spread over first layer. Return to oven and bake for 25 minutes until brown. May be iced with butter icing but if enough cherries can be seen showing through the top, it will look pretty enough as it is. Cut into 36 squares.

ICING

Icing (confectioner's) sugar	1 cup	250 mL
Butter or margarine, softened	2 tbsp.	30 mL
Vanilla	½ tsp.	2 mL
Water or milk	1 tbsp.	15 mL

Beat all together in small bowl adding more water if needed to make a more spreadable mixture. Spread over cooled squares. This makes a minimum amount of frosting.

CHOCOLATE CHIP BARS

Just like a chocolate toffee bar with a fudge coating.

Chocolate cake mix, 2 layer size	1	1
Cooking oil	¼ cup	50 mL
Egg	1	1
Finely chopped walnuts	1 cup	250 mL
Sweetened condensed milk	11 oz.	300 mL
Semisweet chocolate chips	1 cup	250 mL
Vanilla	1 tsp.	5 mL

Combine cake mix, cooking oil, egg and walnuts in mixing bowl. Mix together until crumbly. Reserve 1½ cups (375 mL) for topping. Press remaining mixture into greased 9 x 13 inch (22 x 33 cm) pan.

Put condensed milk, chocolate chips and vanilla into saucepan. Heat and stir to melt chips. Pour over base in pan. Sprinkle with reserved crumbs. Bake in 350°F (180°C) oven for 25 to 30 minutes. Cuts into 54 fairly thin squares.

Pictured on page 197.

This takes a bit more time to make but anything so rich is bound to be worthwhile!

Eggs	2	2
Granulated sugar	¼ cup	50 mL
Brown sugar, packed	1 cup	225 mL
All-purpose flour	¾ cup	175 mL
Baking powder	½ tsp.	2 mL
Vanilla	1 tsp.	5 mL
Salt	⅛ tsp.	0.5 mL
Coconut	½ cup	125 mL
Unsweetened chocolate square, melted	1	1
Butter or margarine, melted	1 tbsp.	15 mL
Chopped walnuts	¼ cup	50 mL
Large marshmallows cut in half (use scissors)	18	18

Beat eggs slightly. Add both sugars, flour, baking powder, vanilla and salt. Stir well. Divide batter into 2 portions.

To 1 part add coconut and mix well. Spread in greased 9 x 9 inch (22 x 22 cm) pan.

To other part add melted chocolate, butter and nuts. Mix and spread over first layer in pan. Bake in 350° F (180° C) oven for 30 minutes or until cooked.

Remove from oven and cover with marshmallow halves, putting 6 one way and 6 along the other making 36 halves in all. Return to oven for 2 minutes. Remove. Use point of knife to spread marshmallows evenly. While still warm, ice with chocolate icing.

ICING

Icing (confectioner's) sugar	1⅓ cups	300 mL
Butter or margarine, softened	2 tbsp.	30 mL
Cocoa	⅓ cup	75 mL
Water	5 tsp.	25 mL

Beat all together in bowl. Add more water if needed so the icing will spread. Smooth over baked squares. Cool. Cut into 36 squares.

TOFFEE OATMEAL BARS

Crunchy chocolate topped squares.

Butter or margarine	⅓ cup	75 mL
Rolled oats	1 cup	225 mL
Brown sugar, packed	½ cup	125 mL
All-purpose flour	½ cup	125 mL
Baking soda	¼ tsp.	1 mL
Chopped walnuts	½ cup	125 mL
Sweetened condensed milk	11 oz.	300 mL
Butter or margarine	2 tbsp.	30 mL
Vanilla	2 tsp.	10 mL
Semisweet chocolate chips	1 cup	250 mL

Melt first amount of butter in medium size saucepan. Stir in rolled oats, brown sugar, flour, baking soda and walnuts. Press into greased 9 x 13 inch (22 x 33 cm) pan. Bake in 350° F (180° C) oven for 10 to 15 minutes until light brown.

Put condensed milk and second amount of butter into clean saucepan. Cook and stir about 15 minutes until it thickens slightly. Remove from heat.

Stir in vanilla. Pour over crust. Return to oven. Bake in 350° F (180° C) oven until golden, about 10 to 15 minutes.

Sprinkle with chocolate chips while hot. Spread when melted. Cuts into 54 fairly thin squares.

Pictured on page 197.

OATMEAL TEAS

So easy to make these good squares. Deep rich color. Contains no flour.

Butter or margarine	½ cup	125 mL
Brown sugar, packed	1 cup	250 mL
Baking soda	1 tsp.	5 mL
Rolled oats	1¾ cups	425 mL

(continued on next page)

Melt butter in medium size saucepan. Stir in sugar. Bring to a boil. Remove from heat.

Add baking soda and stir. Mix in rolled oats. Turn into greased 8 x 8 inch (20 x 20 cm) pan. Bake in 325 °F (160°C) oven for 15 minutes. Remove and quickly cut into squares. Overbaking will make this much too hard. Cuts into 25 squares.

Pictured on page 197.

PEANUT SQUARES

A creamy filling, sandwiched between chocolate layers makes this a rich choice.

FIRST LAYER

Smooth peanut butter	1 cup	250 mL
Semisweet chocolate chips	1 cup	250 mL
Butterscotch chips	1 cup	250 mL

SECOND LAYER

Butter or margarine	½ cup	125 mL
Vanilla custard powder	2 tbsp.	30 mL
Evaporated milk	¼ cup	60 mL
Icing (confectioner's) sugar	3 cups	750 mL
Maple flavoring	½ tsp.	2 mL

THIRD LAYER

Reserved peanut butter mixture		
Peanuts	1 cup	250 mL

First Layer: Combine peanut butter and all chips in saucepan. Heat over low heat stirring often until smooth. Spread ½ mixture over ungreased 9 x 13 inch (22 x 33 cm) pan. Keep second ½ mixture for third layer.

Second Layer: Measure butter, pudding mix and milk in saucepan. Heat and stir until it reaches a full rolling boil. Remove from heat. Add icing sugar and flavoring. Stir well. Spread over first layer.

Third Layer: To reserved mixture add peanuts. Stir and spread over second layer. Chill. Cut into 36 squares.

CHOCOLATE CAROUSELS

This has a peanut butter flavour and looks nice and fruity. While it is usually iced, it is a pretty square without any icing. No baking is required.

Peanut butter	2 cups	500 mL
Icing (confectioner's) sugar	2 cups	500 mL
Butter or margarine	2 tbsp.	30 mL
Salt	1/8 tsp.	0.5 mL
Dates, chopped	1 cup	250 mL
Maraschino cherries, drained and cut	1 cup	250 mL
Chopped pecans or walnuts	1 cup	250 mL

Combine peanut butter, icing sugar, butter and salt in large bowl. Cream together well.

Add dates, cherries and nuts. Stir until mixed. Press into 8 x 8 inch (20 x 20 cm) pan that has been lined with waxed paper. Cover with icing that follows.

ICING

Squares of semisweet chocolate	4	4
Peanut butter	2 tbsp.	30 mL

Melt together slowly in heavy saucepan over low heat. Frost the carousels. Refrigerate. These freeze well and also keep for a lengthy spell in the refrigerator. Cut into 25 squares.

Paré Pointer

Notice how misers don't have much to say? It seems like they don't want to put their two cents in.

METRIC CONVERSION

Throughout this book measurements are given in conventional and metric measure. To compensate for differences between the two measurements due to rounding, a full metric measure is not always used.

The cup used is the standard 8 fluid ounce.

Temperature is given in degrees Fahrenheit and Celsius.

Baking pan measurements are in inches and centimetres, as well as quarts and litres.

An exact conversion is given below as well as the working equivalent.

Spoons	Exact Conversion	Standard Metric Measure
¼ teaspoon	1.2 millilitres	1 millilitre
½ teaspoon	2.4 millilitres	2 millilitres
1 teaspoon	4.7 millilitres	5 millilitres
2 teaspoons	9.4 millilitres	10 millilitres
1 tablespoon	14.2 millilitres	15 millilitres

Cups		
¼ cup (4 T)	56.8 millilitres	50 millilitres
⅓ cup (5⅓ T)	75.6 milliltres	75 millilitres
½ cup (8 T)	113.7 millilitres	125 millilitres
⅔ Cup (10⅔ T)	151.2 millilitres	150 millilitres
¾ cup (12 T)	170.5 millilitres	175 millilitres
1 cup (16 T)	227.3 millilitres	250 millilitres
4½ cups	984.8 millilitres	1000 millilitres, 1 litre

Ounces — Weight		
1 oz.	28.3 grams	30 grams
2 oz.	56.7 grams	55 grams
3 oz.	85 grams	85 grams
4 oz.	113.4 grams	125 grams
5 oz.	141.7 grams	140 grams
6 oz.	170.1 grams	170 grams
7 oz.	198.4 grams	200 grams
8 oz.	226.8 grams	250 grams
16 oz.	453.6 grams	500 grams
32 oz.	917.2 grams	1000 grams, 1 kg.

Pans, Casseroles		
8 x 8-inch	20 x 20 cm, 2L	8 x 2-inch round, 20 x 5 cm, 2L
9 x 9-inch	22 x 22 cm, 2.5 L	9 x 2-inch round, 22 x 5 cm, 2.5L
9 x 13-inch	22 x 33 cm, 4L	10 x 4½-inch tube, 25 x 11 cm, 5L
10 x 15-inch	25 x 38 cm, 1.2L	8 x 4 x 3-inch loaf, 20 x 10 x 7 cm, 1.5L
14 x 17-inch	35 x 43 cm, 1.5L	9 x 5 x 3-inch loaf, 23 x 12 x 7 cm, 2L

Oven Temperatures

Fahrenheit	Celsius	Fahrenheit	Celsius	Fahrenheit	Celsius
175°	80°	300°	150°	425°	220°
200°	100°	325°	160°	450°	230°
225°	110°	350°	180°	475°	240°
250°	120°	375°	190°	500°	260°
275°	140°	400°	200°		

INDEX

222

★ Denotes new recipe

Taste The Tradition

SAVE $5.00

Mail to:
COMPANY'S COMING PUBLISHING LIMITED
BOX 8037, STATION "F"
EDMONTON, ALBERTA, CANADA T6H 4N9

Special Mail Offer: Order any 2 **Company's Coming Cookbooks** by mail at regular prices and **save $5.00** on every third copy per order.   Not valid in combination with any other offer.

Please send the following number of **Company's Coming Cookbooks** to the address on the reverse side of this coupon:

Qty.	Title	Each	Total
	150 DELICIOUS SQUARES	$9.95	
	CASSEROLES	$9.95	
	MUFFINS & MORE	$9.95	
	SALADS	$9.95	
	APPETIZERS	$9.95	
	DESSERTS	$9.95	
	SOUPS & SANDWICHES	$9.95	
	HOLIDAY ENTERTAINING	$9.95	
	COOKIES	$9.95	
	JEAN PARÉ'S FAVORITES VOLUME ONE 232 pages, hard cover	$17.95	
	VEGETABLES (April 1989)	$9.95	
Total Qty.	Total Cost of Cookbooks	$	
	Plus $1.00 postage and handling per copy	$	
Less $5.00 for every third copy per order	— $		
Plus International Shipping Expenses (add $4.00 if outside Canada and U.S.A.)	$		
Total Amount Enclosed	$		

Orders Outside Canada — amount enclosed must be paid in U.S. Funds.

Make cheque or money order payable to: "Company's Coming Publishing Limited"

. . . don't forget to take advantage of the **$5.00 saving** — buy 2 copies by mail and **save $5.00** on every third copy per order.

Prices subject to change after December 31, 1989.

Sorry, no C.O.D.'s.

Taste The Tradition

SAVE $5.00

Mail to:
COMPANY'S COMING PUBLISHING LIMITED
BOX 8037, STATION "F"
EDMONTON, ALBERTA, CANADA T6H 4N9

Special Mail Offer: Order any 2 **Company's Coming Cookbooks** by mail at regular prices and **save $5.00** on every third copy per order.   Not valid in combination with any other offer.

Please send the following number of **Company's Coming Cookbooks** to the address on the reverse side of this coupon:

Qty.	Title	Each	Total
	150 DELICIOUS SQUARES	$9.95	
	CASSEROLES	$9.95	
	MUFFINS & MORE	$9.95	
	SALADS	$9.95	
	APPETIZERS	$9.95	
	DESSERTS	$9.95	
	SOUPS & SANDWICHES	$9.95	
	HOLIDAY ENTERTAINING	$9.95	
	COOKIES	$9.95	
	JEAN PARÉ'S FAVORITES VOLUME ONE 232 pages, hard cover	$17.95	
	VEGETABLES (April 1989)	$9.95	
Total Qty.	Total Cost of Cookbooks	$	
	Plus $1.00 postage and handling per copy	$	
Less $5.00 for every third copy per order	— $		
Plus International Shipping Expenses (add $4.00 if outside Canada and U.S.A.)	$		
Total Amount Enclosed	$		

Orders Outside Canada — amount enclosed must be paid in U.S. Funds.

Make cheque or money order payable to: "Company's Coming Publishing Limited"

. . . don't forget to take advantage of the **$5.00 saving** — buy 2 copies by mail and **save $5.00** on every third copy per order.

Prices subject to change after December 31, 1989.

Sorry, no C.O.D.'s.

GIVE *Company's Coming* TO A FRIEND!

Please send Company's Coming Cookbooks listed on the reverse side of this coupon to:

NAME _____

STREET _____

CITY _____

PROVINCE/STATE _____ POSTAL CODE/ZIP _____

GIFT GIVING — WE MAKE IT EASY!

We will send Company's Coming cookbooks directly to the recipients of your choice — the perfect gift for birthdays, showers, Mother's Day, Father's Day, graduation or any occasion!

Please specify the number of copies of each title on the reverse side of this coupon and provide us with the name and address for each gift order. Enclose a personal note or card and we will include it with your order . . .

. . . and don't forget to take advantage of the **$5.00 saving** — buy 2 copies of **Company's Coming Cookbooks** by mail and **save $5.00** on every third copy per order.

Company's Coming — We Make It Easy — You Make it Delicious!

GIVE *Company's Coming* TO A FRIEND!

Please send Company's Coming Cookbooks listed on the reverse side of this coupon to:

NAME _____

STREET _____

CITY _____

PROVINCE/STATE _____ POSTAL CODE/ZIP _____

GIFT GIVING — WE MAKE IT EASY!

We will send Company's Coming cookbooks directly to the recipients of your choice — the perfect gift for birthdays, showers, Mother's Day, Father's Day, graduation or any occasion!

Please specify the number of copies of each title on the reverse side of this coupon and provide us with the name and address for each gift order. Enclose a personal note or card and we will include it with your order . . .

. . . and don't forget to take advantage of the **$5.00 saving** — buy 2 copies of **Company's Coming Cookbooks** by mail and **save $5.00** on every third copy per order.

Company's Coming — We Make It Easy — You Make it Delicious!

Company's Coming

Taste The Tradition

SAVE $5.00

Mail to:
COMPANY'S COMING PUBLISHING LIMITED
BOX 8037, STATION "F"
EDMONTON, ALBERTA, CANADA T6H 4N9

Special Mail Offer: Order any 2 **Company's Coming Cookbooks** by mail at regular prices and **save $5.00** on every third copy per order.   Not valid in combination with any other offer.

Please send the following number of **Company's Coming Cookbooks** to the address on the reverse side of this coupon:

Qty.	Title	Each	Total
	150 DELICIOUS SQUARES	$9.95	
	CASSEROLES	$9.95	
	MUFFINS & MORE	$9.95	
	SALADS	$9.95	
	APPETIZERS	$9.95	
	DESSERTS	$9.95	
	SOUPS & SANDWICHES	$9.95	
	HOLIDAY ENTERTAINING	$9.95	
	COOKIES	$9.95	
	JEAN PARÉ'S FAVORITES VOLUME ONE 232 pages, hard cover	$17.95	
	VEGETABLES (April 1989)	$9.95	
Total Qty.	Total Cost of Cookbooks	$	
	Plus $1.00 postage and handling per copy	$	
	Less $5.00 for every third copy per order	— $	
	Plus International Shipping Expenses (add $4.00 if outside Canada and U.S.A.)	$	
	Total Amount Enclosed	$	

Orders Outside Canada — amount enclosed must be paid in U.S. Funds.

Make cheque or money order payable to: "Company's Coming Publishing Limited"

. . . don't forget to take advantage of the **$5.00 saving** — buy 2 copies by mail and **save $5.00** on every third copy per order.

Prices subject to change after December 31, 1989.

Sorry, no C.O.D.'s.

GIVE *Company's Coming* TO A FRIEND!

Please send Company's Coming Cookbooks listed on the reverse side of this coupon to:

NAME _____

STREET _____

CITY _____

PROVINCE/STATE _____ POSTAL CODE/ZIP _____

GIFT GIVING — WE MAKE IT EASY!

We will send Company's Coming cookbooks directly to the recipients of your choice — the perfect gift for birthdays, showers, Mother's Day, Father's Day, graduation or any occasion!

Please specify the number of copies of each title on the reverse side of this coupon and provide us with the name and address for each gift order. Enclose a personal note or card and we will include it with your order . . .

. . . and don't forget to take advantage of the **$5.00 saving** — buy 2 copies of **Company's Coming Cookbooks** by mail and **save $5.00** on every third copy per order.

Company's Coming — We Make It Easy — You Make it Delicious!

GIVE *Company's Coming* TO A FRIEND!

Please send Company's Coming Cookbooks listed on the reverse side of this coupon to:

NAME _____

STREET _____

CITY _____

PROVINCE/STATE _____ POSTAL CODE/ZIP _____

GIFT GIVING — WE MAKE IT EASY!

We will send Company's Coming cookbooks directly to the recipients of your choice — the perfect gift for birthdays, showers, Mother's Day, Father's Day, graduation or any occasion!

Please specify the number of copies of each title on the reverse side of this coupon and provide us with the name and address for each gift order. Enclose a personal note or card and we will include it with your order . . .

. . . and don't forget to take advantage of the **$5.00 saving** — buy 2 copies of **Company's Coming Cookbooks** by mail and **save $5.00** on every third copy per order.

Company's Coming — We Make It Easy — You Make it Delicious!